THE BILL

THE OFFICIAL HISTORY OF SUN HILL

THE BILL

THE OFFICIAL HISTORY OF SUN HILL

GEOFF TIBBALLS

CARLTON
BOOKS

This is a Carlton book

This edition first published in Great Britain in 2004 by
Carlton Books Limited
20 Mortimer Street
London W1T 3JW

Text and design copyright © Carlton Books limited, 2003, 2004
Photographs © Fremantle Licensing Limited
The Bill™ Licensed by Fremantle Brand Licensing

The Bill is a trademark of Thames Television Limited. Based on the Thames Television programme *The Bill*.
Licensed by Fremantle Licensing Worldwide. www.thebill.com

Police logos and emblems © Metropolitan Police Authority. Used with permission. www.met.police.co.uk

First published November 2003

Managing Art Director: Jeremy Southgate
Design by Simon Buchanan
Jacket design by Adam Wright
Project Editor Gillian Holmes

ISBN 1 84442 667 X

Printed and bound in Dubai

ACKNOWLEDGEMENTS
Many thanks to the following for making the writing of this book such a pleasurable task: Head of Drama, Thames
Television Paul Marquess, Julie Hill, Continuity Co-ordinator/Archivist (who knows everything there is to know
about *The Bill*), publicists Emily Ogden and Claire Phillips, Jane Foster and Colleen Kay in the picture unit at
Teddington, Beck Eleven at Fremantle Licensing Worldwide, the cast of *The Bill*, and Lorna Russell and Gillian
Holmes at Carlton Books.

CONTENTS

PREVIOUSLY ON
THE BILL

INTRODUCTION

Whisper it softly down at Sun Hill but Reg Hollis and Albert Steptoe have something in common. For just as *Steptoe and Son* stemmed from an episode of the BBC's *Comedy Playhouse*, so *The Bill* originated from a Thames Television showcase for single dramas titled Storyboard. As with *Comedy Playhouse*, the concept of *Storyboard* was that if viewers warmed to a particular episode there was a possibility that it might develop into a series. The Steptoes went on to clean up the mean streets of Shepherd's Bush for 12 years; *The Bill* has been performing a similar service in Sun Hill for 20 years and is still going strong.

It was back in 1983 that Thames producer Michael Chapman was searching for ideas to include in *Storyboard*. Having been impressed by the work of a relatively new writer to television, Geoff McQueen, who had created the successful series *Big Deal* (centred around small-time gambler Robbie Box, played by Ray Brooks) and *Give Us a Break* (set in the

Dave Litten and Jim Carver receive a dressing-down from Sgt Wilding (Peter Dean) in **Woodentop.**

PC 'Taffy' Edwards is seized at gunpoint.

wheeler-dealer world of snooker and starring Robert Lindsay and Paul McGann), Chapman asked McQueen whether he had any other bright ideas. McQueen mentioned *Old Bill*, a project about life in a police station, which had previously been rejected by the BBC. Reworked and given the title *Woodentop* – the nickname bestowed on uniformed officers by CID – the script was directed by Peter Cregeen, who adopted the fly-on-the-wall documentary style of using just one hand-held camera. The programme was transmitted on 16 August 1983 and followed probationary constable Jim Carver's first day at work, the highlight of which was discovering the decomposing body of an old lady in a bath. *Woodentop* received such a good response that within a month a 12-part series was under discussion. There was just one major change to be made: the title would revert to McQueen's original idea, *The Bill*.

McQueen, who died in 1994 at the age of 46, laid down firm foundations for the new series. He decided that events should always be shown from the police point of view so that every scene had to include a police officer. He also made it a rule to steer clear of the officers' domestic lives. 'If they had problems at home,' he told author Hilary Kingsley, 'I wanted to see how it was affecting their work at the station rather than how the work at the station was affecting them at home.'

The first two series of *The Bill* were filmed in Wapping, thereby establishing Sun Hill as being in East London, but the News International industrial dispute of 1985 made even actors in police uniforms unwelcome in the area and forced a move to North Kensington. Then in 1990 production switched to the present base, an industrial estate in Merton.

With first Peter Cregeen, then the returning Michael Chapman, at the helm, *The Bill* enjoyed tremendous success, progressing from a 12-week run in the opening series to a year-round exercise with, from 1993, three half-hour episodes per week. The format continued to change, eventually returning to hour-long episodes, but by 2001 ratings had fallen to just over six million. ITV decided that the show needed rejuvenating. Enter Paul Marquess, formerly series producer of *Brookside*. Old Bill was about to become New Bill.

Under Marquess *The Bill* has changed to a serial format featuring hard-hitting storylines that reflect contemporary policing in London while still retaining the humour that has been part of the show since day one. A wealth of new characters has been introduced and they have proved so popular that within a year viewing figures had increased by 50 per cent, to over nine million.

'I was happy enough at *Brookside*,' says

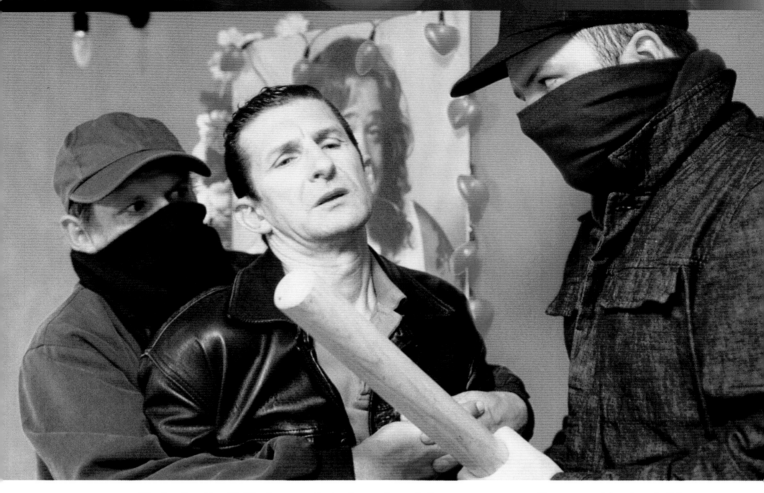

The hapless Reg Hollis discovers that advanced psychology cannot necessarily reason with a baseball bat.

Marquess, 'but I was beginning to think, "I've been here nearly two years, what shall I do next?" Then I got a call from ITV asking whether I wanted to be on the short list to be the new executive producer of *The Bill*. I said, "Yes, I'm always happy to be on a short list". But then a month later I got another call saying: "This short list is very, very short. Why don't you come and see us?" I thought there might be a bit of a problem, for whilst I'd always watched *The Bill*, I hadn't seen it for six months, maybe longer. I'd just fallen out of love with it. So I told ITV that maybe I wasn't the right man for the job, but they said: "No, if you're not watching it, you probably *are* the right man for the job!"

'So I went to London, had a good talk with Thames and with ITV, and clearly the programme had some problems and wasn't performing as well as it had been. The particular problem for ITV as a mass-market channel was that the demographic was getting older and older. It's not that we don't want people over the age of 50 to watch, but for advertising you need a mass audience and that was slipping away. *The Bill* had experimented with doing four and six-part stories, to begin with very successfully – the Fox/Santini storyline was fantastic stuff – but I couldn't quite tell what it had become. As a viewer I didn't know if I switched on whether I was going to get a classic one-off Bill or part three of a four-parter, or part one of a six-parter. The deal you had with *The Bill* whereby you could just watch it when you liked – dip in and out – that deal had changed.

'ITV's prescription was that *The Bill* should become a serial, which obviously required a great deal of thought and hard work. I've

Ted Roach with snout Roxanne (Paul O'Grady).

always said that if someone had argued coherently at that stage for *The Bill* to go back to one-hour, one-off dramas, it might have been just as successful. So I'm not saying that serialisation was the only prescription but if you're going to get me in to do it, that's what you're going to get because my background is working on programmes like *Coronation Street* and *Brookside*. For me, serialisation has delivered a younger audience and a much bigger female audience but I would also argue that our audience has been delivered as much by strong characters as by storytelling. If the characters aren't right, people won't watch.'

On Marquess's second day in the job he made the decision to kill off seven members of the regular cast so that he could bring in new faces.

'*The Bill* has always had strong characters – people like Tosh, Roach, Burnside and Uncle Bob (Cryer) – but when I took over I felt there were either characters who had been here for a long time but weren't being used or other newer characters who hadn't made any discernible hit with the audience, something which often isn't the actor's fault. I compiled my own list of who should go and I went to a meeting with ITV where a research document had been prepared. I hadn't seen the document beforehand but interestingly the names on that list were exactly the same as on mine. I decided that I didn't want seven exits. *The Bill* had become a bit of an exit show – its high points were exits – and Quinnan had just gone, so I thought we'd have one big exit instead.

'The tabloid press like to portray me as an axeman and suggest that I take some sort of pleasure in killing off characters. But that's rubbish. Imagine having to tell seven people in one day that you're not going to renew their contracts – I can assure you it wasn't a day I looked forward to.'

On learning that Sun Hill was about to be wrecked by a petrol bomb and that her character, Kate Spears, was to die in the explosion, actress Tania Emery was resigned to her fate. She said: 'It's better than being sent off to the stationery cupboard and never coming back.'

'Ben Roberts, who played Conway, was equally philosophical about being written out,' says Marquess. 'He said he was amazed it hadn't happened a long time ago. He was one of those I felt had been under-used. We killed

The death toll following the Sun Hill riot of 2002 enabled executive producer Paul Marquess to bring in fresh faces.

Conway a couple of weeks before the others. I was always a Conway fan so we gave him his own explosion. Then we blew up six in one go and just had a memorial service. It worked because it pulled in nine million viewers, although it took us another six months to sustain that level. I had become used as a viewer to tuning in to *The Bill* for a big event, then tuning out again. But now we've got ongoing big events although often the serial element only occupies six scenes per episode.'

A key factor in the rebirth of *The Bill* has been creating and casting plausible, powerful new characters.

Marquess admits: 'It's a hard marketplace and BBC programmes like *Holby City* and *Casualty* use every weapon in the ratings war, including hiring lots of soap stars. I felt *The Bill* had to do the same and do it better. We didn't cast anybody simply because they had been in a soap – that's a complete fallacy. I make no apologies for bringing in ex-soap stars like Todd Carty, Bernie Nolan, Beth Cordingly and Russell Floyd. It helps that they were in these shows but that's not why they're here. I'm interested in good actors. What we did was find good actors and then write parts for them. For example I met Roberta Taylor, who used to be in *Eastenders*, and then I wrote Gina Gold for her, and you can tell it's written for her, which is why she is such a hit with the audience. I'd worked with Diane Parish on Carlton's *Picking Up the Pieces* about five years ago. I phoned her up when she was on a bus. I said: "Do you want to be in *The Bill*?" She said: "Yeah, alright then, luv. Who am I going to play?" I said: "I don't know yet, we'll sort

Todd Carty as the sinister PC Gabriel Kent.

something out." And from that conversation came DC Eva Sharpe.

'Although we now show more of the characters' personal lives, we still don't go home with them. When I got here, they said: "We've got this location for Reg's house that we've leased for a year." They obviously thought the soap element would mean an increase in domesticity but I must have looked horror-stricken. I said: "I don't ever want to go to Reg's house!" In fact I think we went there once when he was kidnapped. Nor for a second did I consider changing the rule regarding the police point of view. It's such a clever idea and a brilliant pre-watershed formula for doing strong stories because the police are hardly ever there when the nasties happen. We do paedophile rings and gang rape, but we don't show it. The big shift is that we now choose stories to illuminate our regular characters. Trudie Goodwin, who plays June Ackland, said to me that she had begun to wonder if she would ever play a new scene again, but now she's had plenty.

'In terms of what goes on in real life, I think if we weren't doing hard-hitting stuff we'd look a bit silly. After all, everybody knows that paedophile rings exist and that children go missing. I'm not looking for a post-watershed slot – I'm happy with the time we go out – and anyway I don't think violence and gore will make people watch *The Bill*. One thing I did, however, was take out a lot of the bad language

The gay kiss between Craig Gilmore and Luke Ashton.

in *The Bill* because that's a real turn-off for parents watching with children.

'Despite the strong storylines we've had hardly any complaints, which means we must be doing things well. In fact since I've been here the only episode about which we did get a stack of complaints was the gay kiss between Luke Ashton and Craig Gilmore. Right from the start I said, "We've got to do a gay kiss before *Merseybeat* does it." They've done one

wasn't in uniform so I got them to do it again. Then for some reason they didn't take any stills, so I got the actors to do the kiss for a third time! Originally I had a different actor in mind for the story but when someone said that Scott Neal, who plays Ashton, wanted to come back, I thought it was a good idea to have someone that the audience recognised among all the new characters we were introducing. I didn't buy the Gilmore character

DC Eva Sharpe (Diane Parish), one of the new officers in **The Bill.**

on *Casualty* but two doctors kissing doesn't have the same impact as two police officers. The joke about our gay kiss was that in meeting after meeting I emphasised that it had to be at the station and it had to be in uniform. But when they did the scene, Luke

at all. I'm gay and here was a copper who was gay and yet it wasn't an issue. I know a lot of gay police officers hated the character and were really insulted by it. I think he was voted Pink Paper villain of the year. In real life gay coppers get a lot of stick from their colleagues

Adam Okaro reflects modern policing in London.

Tom Chandler, moments before turning the gun on himself.

– real horror stories. I didn't think I could change Gilmore completely – Hywel Simons's performance was so strong – but what we did was bring in somebody (Ashton) that really shook him. And that whole storyline made for some great drama.

'When I got here I found that the Met. were ahead of *The Bill*. The Met. have had to change a lot in the wake of the Lawrence inquiry but this wasn't being reflected on screen. Whilst there have always been ethnic officers in *The Bill*, few have been standout characters. Gary McCann was the only one who came close, but I know the Met. are really pleased with the ethnic mix that we've got in the programme now.

'Adam Okaro is a particularly good recruitment model. He's an intensely moral officer – the complete opposite to his predecessor, Tom Chandler. I really like Steven Hartley, who played Chandler, and he did me proud because when Chandler shot himself we got a huge audience. I called Steven in early on and said, "I'm afraid I'm going to have to get rid of Chandler." He said: "Why?" I said: "He's got no moral backbone." The guy at the top has to set the standards and that's what Okaro does.'

In May the murder of Sgt. Matt Boyden was used to launch a new crime series, *MIT*, the initials standing for Murder Investigation Team. 'ITV wanted *The Bill* to kick the new series off,' explains Marquess, 'so the first episode was devoted to solving Boyden's murder. Consequently poor old Boyden was killed twice on screen, once for *The Bill* and once for *M.I.T.*. He was murdered on video on the Thursday night, then murdered on film on the Saturday from a different angle!'

It's certainly been an eventful couple of years at Sun Hill since Paul Marquess took over. 'And there's going to be a real peak this autumn to mark the twenty years,' he says. 'We've enlisted an exciting new series producer, and he's promised to really shake things up...'

TRUDIE GOODWIN

Trudie Goodwin has a confession to make. She's worried about June. 'I'm afraid June's getting a bit of a reputation,' laughs Trudie, 'particularly after she had a one-night stand with Tony Stamp following the break-up with Jim Carver. For years she has been married to the job so that the rest of life has passed her by, but now she seems to be making up for lost time with a vengeance. And I'm afraid she may regret it.

'I think June's always been a secret raver but she's managed to keep her work and private life separate. She is, after all, dedicated to the job. The trouble is, she's not very good at picking the right man.

'In the old days we weren't allowed to do

in Australia who proposed to me in a letter. I explained that I was married with kids but he didn't give up easily and still sends me postcards. At the other extreme, I get lots of letters from young girls who want me to be their mum.'

She also gets a good reaction from real

INTERVIEW

anything about our characters' personal lives although we used to try and sneak little personal things in like saying how many sugars she'd take in her tea. So I must admit I was shocked to learn June would be having a relationship with Jim — as was Mark Wingett. It was something neither of us had envisaged and it was quite difficult to make it work, although thankfully there were no steamy sex scenes!'

Trudie is married to actor/writer Kit Jackson (they have two daughters) but this hasn't stopped viewers who have fallen in love with June proposing marriage to her. 'I did have one persistent suitor a rich old man

police officers. 'The police often wave to me or stop and have a chat. They'll tell me if there's a parking space around the corner. I think that's because June's a good role model for the police.

June Ackland and Nick Shaw bring in a suspect.

as Sgt. June Ackland

Born in Eltham, south-east London, Trudie has been in *The Bill* since the start yet she very nearly didn't bother attending the audition for the single play *Woodentop*. 'I'd never played a policewoman before – I usually played the wife of someone dodgy – so I nearly didn't go because I thought it would be a waste of time. Also I'd got a new baby and it meant trailing right across London, but my husband persuaded me to go. When I walked in, I said, "I know I'm not what you're looking for." And they said I didn't look like my photo in

Spotlight, which was true because it was an old picture and also I'd put on a bit of weight with the pregnancy. So I got home thinking that was pointless and then the phone rang to say I'd got the part!'

Among Trudie's most rewarding storylines over the past 20 years was an episode dealing with a cot death victim. 'That was very moving and quite harrowing and for years afterwards it was used as training for police officers having to deal with infant death syndrome. I also enjoyed the story where my flat was burned down – it made a change to get from behind my desk.'

However there have been times when Trudie longed to be in the warmth and safety of the studio. 'I hate rain machines. Once I got so

soaked that all the dye came out of my uniform and my underwear turned blue. And when you're doing night shoots in February for transmission in July, you have to wear summer clothing and it can get very cold. It really is no fun being up to your thighs in the Thames in winter.

'I ended up in hospital once after running headlong into a stunt man during a chase sequence but my worst experience was with an Alsatian. The dog was meant to jump out at June and Taffy Edwards as we were walking past a factory. The dog, which was chained to a wall, had been trained to attack the uniform and to prove the point when it was shown the uniform before the first take it went absolutely mad. On the first two takes, the dog leaped out snarling and everything was fine but on the third take the chain broke. As the dog came hurtling towards us, the trainer screamed at us to freeze. We dared not move a muscle and luckily the dog stopped three feet away from us. But it was very scary.'

THE HISTORY
OF SUN HILL

THE GINGER NINJA

Detective Inspector Roy Galloway liked to run a tight ship – but sometimes the only thing that was tight around Sun Hill was his DS, Ted Roach. The two men had more in common than either would probably care to admit. Galloway possessed a temper to match his fiery hair but usually reserved it for withering verbal attacks on Uniform, whom he generally perceived as at best, incompetent and, at worst, obstructive. The hard-drinking Roach was equally volatile but sometimes expressed his anger with his fists, which explained why he was still a DS and never likely to climb any higher. Whilst neither man was likely to win too many popularity contests around the station, they were both damned good thief-takers.

Where they differed was in their approach to women. Ted's surname said it all. He would chase anything with a pulse (and that was only preferable rather than compulsory), chatting up whoever crossed his path, including suspects. He thought it was normal practice, a perk of the job, and when a fellow officer suggested otherwise, an incredulous Roach asked: 'Have you never slept with a bird you've nicked?' Galloway, however, saw women as the bane of his life. If they weren't giving him grief at home, they were getting on his nerves at the station. When June Ackland found the body of a missing teenage girl, she informed Galloway, unaware that he was taking his first day off for months. She was so upset by his rudeness that she seriously considered chucking the job in, all the more so when he accused her of not doing her job properly. For June it was a salutary reminder of the harsh, chauvinistic

world of CID, where the only approachable figure was smooth DC Mike Dashwood, disparagingly described by Roach as 'a grammar school ponce'. Ted didn't like people who were better educated than him, a sentiment which therefore put him at loggerheads with most of the population.

Galloway could have invented the term 'road rage'. On one occasion he was so angry after being given a parking ticket that when he proceeded to bump into a taxi, he promptly arrested the driver. Within the hour the roads around Sun Hill were jammed by protesting taxi drivers but Galloway flatly refused to drop the case. Eventually he was ordered to do so in the interests of public safety. He was grumpier than ever that night.

An Unwelcome Visitor
Visiting detectives from other patches were

>**16 August 1983**
Transmission of single drama *Woodentop*

>**16 October 1984**
First episode under title *The Bill* features a neighbouring nick's Sgt. Tommy Burnside (as he was then known)

>**23 October 1984**
DS Ted Roach makes his debut

Chalk and cheese: Ted Roach and Mike Dashwood.

>20 November 1984
Four years before playing, PC Tony Stamp, actor Graham Cole appears as an uncredited background extra in the episode 'The Drugs Raid'

>22 January 1985
PC Dave Litten leaves Sun Hill

>3 February 1986
PC Viv Martella keeps goal for the Sun Hill five-a-side football team. PC Jim Carver has to miss the match after spraining his ankle chasing muggers

Dave Litten (right) tries to copy the style of his boss, Roy Galloway.

guaranteed to put Galloway's back up almost as quickly as women and taxi drivers. Take Burnside, a hard-nosed DS with a reputation for cutting more corners than Nigel Mansell. Long-serving desk sergeant Bob Cryer couldn't believe that Burnside had slipped through the net of Operation Countryman, the covert investigation designed to trap bent coppers in the Met. He was not alone in his misgivings. Galloway was none too keen on Burnside either so when the latter breezed into Sun Hill demanding the release of a prisoner, sparks flew. The bone of contention was a car thief by the name of Lennie who had been caught in the act by PCs Jim Carver and

'Taffy' Edwards. Burnside told Galloway that Lennie was a snout who was needed back on the streets as part of a major operation. Galloway wasn't happy about it and he and Burnside exchanged a few choice words, but in the end he was faced with no alternative. Since it was his first arrest, Carver was furious to hear that Lennie was being freed and he

SUN HILL – *The Facts*

Peter Dean, who went on to play stallholder Pete Beale in EastEnders, appeared as Sgt. Wilding in Woodentop, the pilot programme for The Bill.

>7 December 1987
Sgt. Tom Penny is shot in the stomach by an old lady

Bob Cryer finds himself on the wrong end of a sawn-off shotgun.

confronted Cryer for an explanation. Cryer said that sometimes the rules have to be bent to catch bigger fish. As Carver licked his wounds and headed back out on patrol, he saw Burnside drive past with a passenger. It was Lennie, looking very pleased with himself. This was Jim Carver's first taste of Burnside. There would be many more to come.

Burnside also put in an appearance at the retirement party for

Fresh-faced young bobbies
June Ackland and
Jim Carver.

Reg Hollis prides himself on his uncanny knack of being first on the scene.

Chief Superintendent Brownlow's clerk, a post coveted by earnest young PC Reg Hollis. Refreshments were served in a room above a pub, the supply boosted by a consignment of stolen Scotch that mysteriously turned up behind the bar. Ted Roach took full advantage of the situation, drove home blind drunk and crashed his car into someone's front garden. He then tried to wriggle off the hook by promising to get the householder into the Specials. Hollis reported the incident to Brownlow in the hope that it would help his application for the vacant clerk's position, but Roach managed to save his skin by striking lucky with a gang of suede coat thieves. Some say he got his comeuppance 18 months later when he was stabbed in the backside by a group of louts in a pub.

The Ambitious Dave Litten

One man who ultimately had his eyes on Ted Roach's job was PC Dave Litten. Desperate to join CID and exert his superiority over the Uniform woodentops, Litten pulled out all the stops to impress Galloway and was rewarded with a temporary secondment. However, it wasn't long before he felt the rough edge of Galloway's tongue. Investigating the theft of a valuable necklace, Litten relied on the word of a snout who contacted him by telephone to say that he could point out the burglars. In fact he was only interested in the reward money and led Litten to two innocent suspects, but by the time the rookie detective realised he'd been set up, the wheels of justice were in motion. Galloway had to intervene to stop Litten making an even bigger fool of himself. A couple of weeks later Boy Blunder struck again, when he handed a car from the pound over to someone who wasn't the rightful owner. Litten's failure to ask for ID resulted in another reprimand from Galloway. He still had a lot to learn.

The Trials and Tribulations of Bob Cryer

Life was not exactly plain sailing for Bob Cryer, particularly after the arrival of a stern new inspector, Brian Kite, who wanted to shake up Uniform. As well as dealing with his own problems – such as when he knocked down and killed an old lady in bad weather – Bob had to keep a watchful eye on the more wayward members of his relief. Prominent among these was PC Pete Muswell, whose taunting of the station's first black officer, Abe Lyttleton, got so out of hand that Cryer felt obliged to take him to one side during a football match between Sun Hill and a local youth club and warn him about his behaviour. That was a bad day all round for the station: with WPC Viv Martella in goal they lost 5-2.

Then there was Bob's fellow sergeant, Tom Penny. A bit of a moaner, Tom was never the easiest person to work with, but even Bob was shocked when Mrs Penny asked him for help because Tom was beating her up. Things got worse when Tom went to investigate a seemingly routine complaint from a landlord about a local mad woman who kept a posse of cats in her flat. Suddenly the woman produced a gun and shot Penny in the stomach. Trapped in the flat out of reach of his radio, it looked grim for Penny but fortunately he was found in the nick of time and rushed to hospital. However, he would never be the same again.

Out of the blue at the end of 1987 Galloway decided to move on. Although the two had their differences over the years, Cryer was sorry to see him go. He was even sorrier on discovering who Galloway's permanent replacement would be.

JEFF STEWART

Unlikely as it may sound, Reg Hollis used to hang out with James Bond! Or rather Jeff Stewart was friendly with Pierce Brosnan when the pair were students together at the Drama Centre in Chalk Farm, north London. Yet it was by no means Stewart's first claim to fame. As a three-year-old he had won a certificate in a school acting competition for his expert impersonation of a fish. Clearly there is more to Reg Hollis than meets the eye.

'Pierce and I lived two streets apart,' recalls Stewart, 'so we used to travel home together. Even then I could see that he had the potential to become a major star because he went to such trouble over everything. He brought West End values to a drama school production. I

over Benny in *Crossroads*. 'About a year later I received a cheque for £14. It was a repeat fee. Benny had apparently remembered the accident in a dream sequence.'

When Stewart, whose own voice betrays no hint of Reg's nasal whine, was first sent

INTERVIEW

bumped into him about ten years ago in the King's Road and we chatted about the old days.'

Born in Aberdeen, Stewart was educated in Hampshire. 'I wanted to act before I knew what acting was,' he says. He spent two years at the Drama Centre but a chance meeting in a pub led to a job as an assistant stage manager in the West End. With his Equity card secured, he appeared in a number of TV series, most notably as evil thug Harry Fellows, who ran

Hollis heard a search was on for a Bin Laden.

along to casting sessions for *The Bill*, he was told by the director Peter Cregeen that there was nothing really suitable for him. 'I had long hair and a beard at the time. Peter had all the character descriptions spread out on his desk and although he told me he thought I was a smashing fellow, I didn't fit any of them. We talked for about 20 minutes and I was just about to leave when he remembered Hollis, whose voice had been heard over the radio in *Woodentop* but who had not

as PC Reg Hollis

actually been seen. So he said, "We could bring Hollis to life in the shape of you.'" Stewart was initially promised just one episode; he and Hollis have been at Sun Hill ever since.

Not surprisingly, Stewart has developed quite a soft spot for Reg. 'I love the man to bits and he's great fun to play, a sort of gold Amex card of the poetic licence world because I can do anything with him. He is funny without knowing it and that makes him a gift to an actor. I've been lucky that I've been given great freedom to develop Hollis. They give me the eggs and a whisk

and it's up to me whether I spill it or make an omelette! He's not based on anyone in particular but I incorporate things that I see in people. And I love working with props where I can add my own idiosyncratic take so that a scene with Reg can, I hope, sometimes be like a silent comedy.

'I enjoy playing the underdog and although he's a bit of a clown, he never completely messes up. When he was kidnapped, initially he had no idea why he had been taken but his professionalism kicked in. He used his head, considered his opponent and realised that rule number one was "establish a relationship with the kidnapper". Charlie Lawson, who played the kidnapper, was brilliant and the

sight of Reg up against this formidable man worked really well.'

Hollis's popularity is borne out by the amount of fan mail Stewart receives. 'A lot of actors from outside *The Bill* tell me how much they enjoy Reg. Even Tony Blackburn is a Hollis fan. Most of the letters I get are very sweet. I had one from a lady in New York who had seen an episode with Reg in particularly sympathetic mood and was obviously quite

taken with him. It was almost a proposal of marriage. I just sent back a photo. It's strange, I always jump to his defence, but the viewers really do like Reg even if he is a bit of an oddball. But then perhaps that's why he is so popular. He's not perfect but he is very human and people can relate to that.'

FEARLESS FRANK

It was all change at Sun Hill at the start of 1988. Not only had Galloway gone but so had Kite. Ted Roach was appointed acting DI and the new Uniform inspector, Christine Frazer (having quickly fallen for Ted's unsubtle charms), wanted the promotion to be made permanent but was informed that Brownlow would never recommend it. Instead the job went to Frank Burnside. Bob Cryer was appalled and began bad-mouthing Burnside until Frazer, 'an old mate' of Frank's, put him straight. Roach hid his disappointment in the way he knew best – by buying his new guv'nor a drink.

Burnside set out his stall at once, telling his CID staff that he would back them all the way so long as they didn't take him for a mug. They soon learned that this was wise advice, for when it came to nursing grudges Frank was in the Florence Nightingale class. Remembering how shady solicitor Julian Pembridge had once bent the rules to keep a dangerous villain

'Yorkie' Smith looks on as Frank Burnside tries to control the wayward Ted Roach.

> **19 July 1988**
Format switches from hour-long episodes to half-hours, screened twice weekly

> **4 August 1988**
Frank Burnside arrives at Sun Hill as the new DI

> **27 October 1988**
DC 'Tosh' Lines makes his first appearance

Christine Frazer enjoyed a 'special relationship' with CID.

like a police informer. He then sat back and watched while Simpson was given a sound beating by his fellow villains.

Since Burnside chose to sail close to the wind, he was bound to run into the occasional storm. He had crossed swords with so many people – on both sides of the law — that they were almost queuing up to take a pop at him. Chief Superintendent Pearson, who had once served as a DC under Burnside, tried to frame him in connection with Operation Backwoods, a corruption inquiry. Found in possession of a carrier bag containing £2,000 – the alleged payment for a prisoner's parole application – Burnside had to think fast and used new recruit DC 'Tosh' Lines as his legman to prove that the whole thing was a stitch-up instigated by Pearson. Apparently Pearson had wanted to get even with Burnside for swindling him out of some money years ago. From then on, Burnside always had a soft spot for Lines – well, as soft as a man like Burnside ever got.

Christine Frazer's Dangerous Liaison

Although Burnside had tried early on to wind Cryer up by telling him he was going to get the nick sorted, relations between CID and Uniform profited from the 'special relationship' that Frazer enjoyed with the station's two senior detectives. Happily divorced, Burnside had once enjoyed a fling with Frazer and was keen to rekindle the romance but instead she opted for Roach. Ted needed cheering up. Failing a firearms refresher course meant that he was no longer entitled to carry a gun. It was

called Barry Dwyer at liberty, Burnside planted a vanload of video recorders outside Pembridge's house. Pembridge rose to the bait by helping himself to one of the recorders but the trap backfired when a furious Brownlow stepped in and ordered Burnside to back off. Pembridge was released with a caution. But Burnside was not to be denied when exacting revenge on another old adversary, a security guard named Simpson, whom he had nicked six years earlier for robbery with violence. Investigating alone a possible break-in at an industrial plant, Burnside was knocked unconscious by the waiting Simpson but got his own back by setting up the guard to look

> 21 March 1989
The 100th episode of *The Bill* – titled 'A Death in the Family'

> 25 July 1989
Death of PC Pete Ramsey

> 15 August 1989
PC Tony 'Yorkie' Smith takes a security job up north

The three degrees: Bob Cryer, Steve Loxton and Derek Conway undergo firearms training.

SUN HILL – *The Facts*

A world away from Frank Burnside, actor Chris Ellison has illustrated children's books written by his former co-star on The Bill, Tom Cotcher (DC Alan Woods).

a serious career blow, although he confided to Sadie, his favourite barmaid, that he had always had a dread of 'blowing somebody away'. Initially Burnside observed the Frazer/Roach affair with detached amusement. Before their opening date he told Roach not to expect too much from that first night but to be prepared

to hit the jackpot on the second. However, as the unlikely liaison developed, Burnside couldn't help sticking his oar in, probably out of jealousy. He told Frazer to ditch Roach, saying that she could 'do better', meaning him. Frazer replied that it was none of his business but Burnside insisted that it was his business if Roach's work was beginning to suffer. When Chief Inspector Conway heard about the affair, he warned Roach that if it didn't end he would be transferred to another division. Roach rounded on his CID colleagues for grassing him up but Burnside had little sympathy and

> **21 December 1989**
PC Dave Quinnan's first day at Sun Hill

> **11 January 1990**
Insp. Christine Frazer and PC 'Taffy' Edwards say farewell to Sun Hill

> **27 March 1990**
Viv Martella moves from Uniform to CID

told Roach he had behaved like a prat.

The dalliance with Frazer gave Roach a taste for inspectors and encouraged him to apply for promotion. Arriving at Hendon for the promotion board, he discovered that his interview had been re-scheduled for the afternoon so he and another candidate adjourned to the pub for lunch. It was a fatal move. Not for the first time (or the last), Ted got involved in a brawl with a customer and ended up being head-butted. Turning up for the interview dripping in blood, he was not altogether surprised to learn that his application was unsuccessful. He was so disenchanted that he was on the point of resigning until Burnside managed to talk him out of it.

Frazer came out of the affair only marginally better. Conway didn't take to her at all and she further jeopardised her prospects of advancement by failing to control her team during a mock riot exercise at a training centre – a blunder that was reported back to Sun Hill. With her job on the line, she came up before Brownlow for appraisal and took the opportunity to vent her frustrations as a female officer, naming Conway as the major stumbling block. Caught between a rock and a hard place, Brownlow took Conway's side, leaving Frazer with little alternative other than to resign. Before leaving, she told Burnside good-naturedly that he was a lecherous, conniving bastard with a vicious streak. Frank was flattered.

Sgt. Alec Peters, reeling from a knife wound after being stabbed by a junkie.

A Period of Mourning

Christine Frazer was not the only casualty. Tom Penny never completely recovered from the shooting and turned to drink. Stitched up by officers from Barton Street, who breathalysed him in retaliation for one of their men being reported for assaulting a prisoner, Penny chose to resign on medical grounds. The following year another Uniform sergeant, Alec Peters, was stabbed by a junkie on the Whitegate Estate and sustained such serious injuries that he was moved upstairs out of the firing line. Nor would anybody at Sun Hill forget the day

> **22 May 1990**
PC Ken Melvin is killed by car bomb

> **31 May 1990**
The newly refurbished Sun Hill station is officially opened

> **30 October 1990**
Sgt. Bob Cryer shoots dead an armed robber

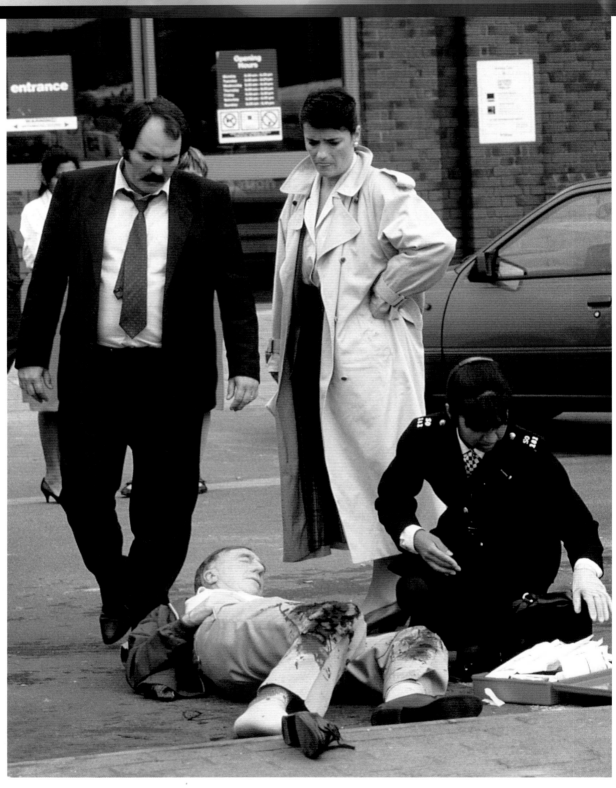

'Tosh' Lines and Viv Martella survey the carnage.

> **31 October 1991**
PC Phil Young commits suicide

> **7 November 1991**
A new sergeant, Matt Boyden, arrives at
Sun Hill

when 'Tosh' Lines's chaotic domestic existence inadvertently cost a young officer his life. It has to be said that PC Pete Ramsey wasn't everyone's cup of tea. He had a condescending sneer, drove around in a Porsche and marked his first day by speeding away from a garage without paying for petrol. Unfortunately for Ramsey, the garage owner was a friend of Bob Cryer's. Ramsey led a charmed life until the day that Tosh's wife Muriel decided to cause a disturbance at a bank. She made such a fuss that Tosh was ordered to go and deal with her, but before he arrived, the bank was raided by armed robbers. Everyone inside was held hostage, including Mrs Lines and her children. Desperate to rescue his family, Tosh tried to burst into the bank but was prevented from doing so by Ramsey, who had been sent to the scene. In the commotion Ramsey was gunned down by one of the raiders. Tosh was scarcely

SUN HILL – *The Facts*

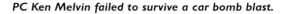

Tony Scannell, who played the brawling DS Ted Roach, was himself beaten up two weeks before joining **The Bill** *while trying to rescue an old lady from two muggers.*

cheered by his annual performance appraisal from Conway, who described him as 'fat, unfit and unambitious'.

The summer of 1990 was particularly traumatic for Sun Hill. With the long-awaited opening of the refurbished station a matter of days away, popular PC Ken Melvin was killed by a car bomb. Even Burnside was moved and arranged for CID to devote their energies to a minor case so that they would be able to attend the funeral. Under Brownlow's awkward leadership, the VIP opening ceremony went ahead, although Burnside found an excuse to be elsewhere. There was a minor

PC Ken Melvin failed to survive a car bomb blast.

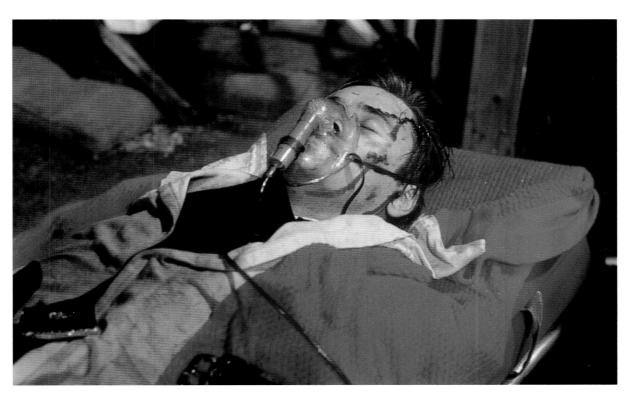

The riot squad are called out to restore order to the streets of Sun Hill.

embarrassment when the party stumbled across a dishevelled Lines in one of the portakabins, munching an apple on all fours, and as the mayor came to cut the ribbon, nobody could find any scissors. But these hiccups paled into insignificance when the speeches were interrupted by a man claiming to have found a dead body on Canley Fields. It was that of eight-year-old Jennie Price. She had been strangled and the only clue was the dog hair found on her clothing. Detective Superintendent Jack Meadows from AMIP (Area Major Incident Pool) was called in and immediately linked the murder with that of another child, Graeme Butler, also found dead on Canley Fields just a few weeks earlier. With the local paper criticising Sun Hill's failure to catch the double killer, suspicion fell on Peter Angell, the caretaker at Norse Hill Primary School where Graeme was a pupil. A keen dog walker, Angell had once been accused of assaulting young children, but he had a strong alibi and was released. A few weeks later PC Dave Quinnan was visiting a local primary school that had been broken into when he noticed a man with a large soft toy dog dressed in red, talking to a group of children. His name was Donald Blake and he was giving a talk about 'dogs in danger', assisted by his mascot, 'Mervyn the Mongrel. Quinnan suddenly remembered that a wino, interviewed as a witness during the murder inquiry, had described seeing 'a big dog in a red coat driving a car'. Roach scoffed at the lead, pointing out that the same wino had later claimed to have seen 'a black panther driving a bus', but Quinnan persevered and discovered that Blake had visited Jennie Price's school on the day before her murder. Seemingly relieved to have been caught, Blake confessed and Quinnan was put forward for a commendation.

It was a timely boost for Quinnan's career. On first arriving at Sun Hill, he had been reprimanded by the ever-vigilant Inspector Andrew Monroe (Frazer's successor) for selling calculators to other officers. To exacerbate the situation, the crime figures that Monroe had asked collator Cathy Marshall to compile for Brownlow were distorted because the calculator she'd bought from Quinnan was faulty!

Fortunately for Quinnan, the new Area Car driver, Steve Loxton, was on hand to monopolise most of the complaints, whether it was for upsetting the public, intimidating suspects or reckless driving. With Loxton at the wheel, the Sun Hill yard resembled a scene from Demolition Derby.

Bob Cryer prepares to face the consequences.

Bob Cryer's Nightmare

It wasn't only the younger officers who found themselves under investigation. Bob Cryer's worst nightmare occurred when he and Stamp were authorised, as firearms officers, to attend the scene of a building society robbery in which a security guard was shot. The gang made their escape, only to find their route to an industrial estate blocked by two police cars.

DCI Gordon Wray was transferred after a fling with Ackland.

One of the robbers, Harris, leaped from the getaway car brandishing a sawn-off shotgun and shot Stamp, whereupon Cryer fired back after first shouting a warning. As Harris lay dead on the ground, a sombre Cryer was informed that he had not been in any danger because Harris had run out of ammunition. However, he could not have known that. As if Cryer hadn't been through enough for one day, Reg Hollis offered to represent him at the inevitable inquiry. Always eager to distance himself from controversy, Brownlow advised

SUN HILL – *The Facts*

Graham Cole (PC Tony Stamp) reckons he has been pulled over by the police about a dozen times over the years. 'It scares the hell out of me,' he admits. 'I know I haven't done anything wrong, but I pull over and they say, "Can you sign this for my wife?"'

Cryer to take some time off. In the light of the adverse publicity surrounding his shooting of an 'unarmed' man, Cryer felt that he had become a political liability, an opinion shared by the spineless Brownlow, who suggested that it might be better if he were transferred away from Sun Hill. But Conway and Monroe disagreed and persuaded Cryer to stay.

June Makes her Mark
June Ackland took the unusual step of bringing a private prosecution against a member of the public. While trying to arrest a drug pusher on the Jasmine Allen Estate, June was punched and kicked by the estate's 'community representative', Everton Warwick. However, the Crown Prosecution Service declined to bring a charge of GBH against Warwick for fear of upsetting the delicate balance on the estate and so June took the law into her own hands, only to lose the case and finish up both financially and

SUN HILL – *The Facts*

On joining The Bill *as PC Ron Smollett, actor Nick Stringer was told to shave off his moustache so that he could be distinguished from Kevin Lloyd, who played 'Tosh' Lines.*

Reg Hollis gets to grips before a gunman (played by Roger Lloyd Pack) can pull the trigger.

SUN HILL – *The Facts*

*On-screen lovers Lisa Geoghan
(Polly Page) and Andrew Paul
(Dave Quinnan) have been firm friends since
attending stage school together.*

SUN HILL – *The Facts*

*In 1990 Philip Whitchurch played Barton
Street inspector Philip Twist but when he
joined Sun Hill three years later, the
inspector's surname had changed to Cato.*

Kim Reid was keen to see the back of Burnside.

emotionally drained.

June was also a pivotal figure in the short-lived Sun Hill career of DCI Gordon Wray, brought in to supervise Burnside. The two men were at daggers drawn from the outset, and their views on policing were poles apart. Wray laid down the law on his first day in the job, telling Burnside that 'Jack-the-lad' methods were out, crime management was in. Burnside continued to resent Wray's presence until Roach hinted that Wray was enjoying a bit on the side with Ackland. This earned Wray a degree of respect from Burnside, who had always seen him as a bit of a boy scout but now viewed him in a different light. Winning Burnside's approval was to prove small consolation because once Mrs Wray found out about the affair, the DCI was quickly transferred.

The Reign of Kim Reid

Gordon Wray's replacement was DCI Kim Reid, who found Burnside so difficult to monitor that she tried to get him promoted in order to be rid of him. Meanwhile Burnside had weightier matters on his mind, having come under investigation by the Serious Crime Squad over the murder of 'supergrass' Lennie Powell, shot dead outside a Sun Hill safe house. The implication was that Burnside had passed information to the killer, a suspicion hardened by the fact that Burnside alone had ordered extra police protection to be stood down following an earlier unsuccessful attempt on Powell's life. Feeling the heat, Burnside asked Roach to say that they had both agreed to stand down the extra cover, but when Roach refused to play ball and told the truth, the pair became involved in an unseemly brawl that was only broken up by the intervention of Reid, Lines and Carver. Reid ordered Frank to shape up or ship out.

Burnside survived that threat to his career but predictably enough the next one was not far behind. A small-time villain, Tony 'Gonzo'

SUN HILL – *The Facts*

Martin Marquez, who played DS Danny Pearce, used to run his own fish and chip shop.

Jack Meadows' patience would be sorely tested in years to come by DS Debbie McAllister.

Brooks, told CID that a contract killer was about to make a 'hit' in Sun Hill. Burnside dismissed this as fantasy but Reid took the precaution of notifying AMIP, which brought Jack Meadows in on the action. When 'Gonzo' turned out to be the victim, Meadows blasted Burnside for his handling of the affair and warned him that if he didn't find the killer – and fast – his career was finished.

The successful solution of that case combined with Reid's promotion and departure promised to open new doors for Burnside but an interview board at Scotland Yard for the position of DCI came to grief.

Burnside wondered whether Reid had put the boot in as a farewell gift. But then came the really bad news. Meadows was to be his new boss.

SUN HILL – *The Facts*

Rene Zagger, who plays PC Nick Klein, has an elder brother who is a policeman. When Zagger won his part in The Bill, his brother invited him to spend a week with Essex Constabulary, where he saw plenty of action, including a brawl involving 200 people.

SIMON ROUSE

Hard men Jack Meadows and Frank Burnside may have come across as the best of enemies on screen, each trying to outglare the other, but actors Simon Rouse and Chris Ellison spent most of their scenes together falling about laughing. 'I used to be a terrible corpser,' admits Simon, 'and it was worse when Chris was around. He always used to make me laugh. Usually I would start cracking up at the absurdity of me trying to act tough, when I am not at all authoritarian in real life. I remember once I had to turn to some lowlife and say, "Do you make a habit of battering frail old-age pensioners?" and as I said it I had this surreal vision of them all being lined up. That set me off.'

Simon, who is married to former *Father, Dear Father* actress Annie Holloway (now a successful artist), says he has learned a lot

realised that you don't have to shout to convey authority. He no longer has to rant and rave to announce that he's a DCI – it can all be done

INTERVIEW

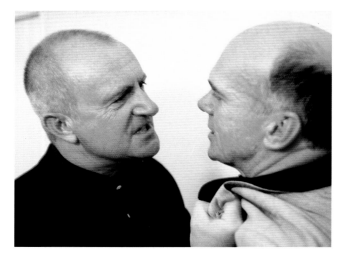

Meadows gets tough.

with a look, the tone of his voice or just the way he carries himself. I can't be doing a bad job because when I meet real DCIs they're pretty complimentary. The fantastic thing is that I've had time to develop the character. In a way it's been like one long rehearsal and now Paul Marquess has given Meadows some great storylines, allowing the character to be fleshed out.

'Mind you, I never take anything for granted. The option on our contracts comes up every six months so I just treat the job as six months' work at a time without looking too far ahead.'

Simon clearly has a healthy respect for Meadows. 'He's a really professional cop, a straight guy. He has his faults but I like that.

about authority through playing Meadows for over 11 years. 'I've made him much less irascible than he was at first because I've

as DCI Jack Meadows

One of his problems is that he lives for his job and since his split from wife Laura I think he's been lonely. In company with most men he likes women but he tends to fall head over heels in love. Behind that tough exterior he's quite a romantic but this leaves him vulnerable and susceptible to the charms of a beautiful woman like Debbie McAllister. It was a good twist that in the end he didn't get off with Debbie but she treated him very badly and I don't think he'll forget that.'

Simon says one of his favourite episodes was

Bradford-born Simon knew he wanted to be an actor as a teenager. He started doing school plays from the age of 12 and after attending drama school appeared in various film and TV productions, invariably on the wrong side of the law. In *Coronation Street* he played a vengeful husband who beat up Mike Baldwin and in *Bread* he was a local villain intent on scaring the hell out of Joey Boswell.

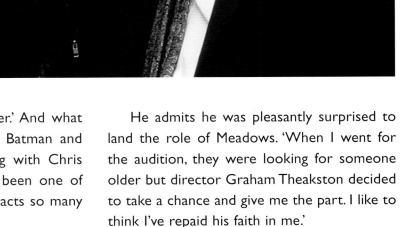

the 1995 story 'Mitigating Circumstances', in which he had to interview Ray Winstone who was playing crook Jack Mackenzie. 'That was really powerful stuff, but I also enjoyed all the episodes I did with Chris Ellison and with Steven Hartley who managed to turn Tom Chandler into a thoroughly dislikeable character.' And what about Meadows and Webb, the Batman and Robin of Sun Hill? 'Yes, working with Chris Simmons was great, too. That's been one of the pleasures of *The Bill* — it attracts so many fine actors.'

He admits he was pleasantly surprised to land the role of Meadows. 'When I went for the audition, they were looking for someone older but director Graham Theakston decided to take a chance and give me the part. I like to think I've repaid his faith in me.'

CHANGING FACES

If Burnside was none too thrilled to discover that Jack Meadows was his new DCI, he was in good company. For Meadows himself was still seething at having been busted down from superintendent after his bagman Lovell was found guilty of corruption. It was the injustice that rankled. There was no suggestion that Meadows was corrupt, his only crime being one of inadequate supervision, although the whole business did put a question mark against his judgement of character.

As he looked around his inherited staff on his first day at Sun Hill, there were plenty of characters to judge. There was Burnside, who demonstrated his resentment at being overlooked for the job by 'forgetting' to give Meadows the key to his office. Thus the new head of CID found himself ignominiously stranded in the corridor. It was scarcely a

Inspector Monroe calms a heated situation before Loxton or Garfield can make things worse.

>**24 March 1992**
Jack Meadows' first day as a DCI at Sun Hill

>**2 July 1992**
DC Mike Dashwood is transferred to the Art and Antiques Squad

>**24 December 1992**
The story 'Return Match' marks the 500th episode of The Bill

Marshall, Quinnan, Stamp and Garfield use minimum force.

promising start to their working relationship. There was the elegant and articulate Mike Dashwood, something of a fish out of water; jolly Jim Carver, the Grim Reaper in a suit; Viv Martella, enthusiastic but still learning, like an untrained Labrador; 'Tosh' Lines, whose fitness level confined his collars to asthmatics and amputees; Alistair Greig, friendly enough on the surface, but was he really a team player? And last but not least Ted Roach, still hanging on, still crazy after all these years.

Going, Going...

Dashwood was the first to leave, striking out to pursue art thieves. The Detective Constable was about to become a Constable detective. Others would soon be following him through the exit door.

Quite apart from the missing key, Meadows' initial impact was not what he would have hoped. The station was full of gossip about his demotion, and when he heard

Loxton casting aspersions, he forced the young upstart to apologise. He soon faced a more serious threat to his authority, but at least it gave him the chance to make his mark – to show Brownlow and Conway how *he* wanted to police Sun Hill. Trouble was brewing on the local estates. Just a fortnight after a full-scale riot had been narrowly averted on the Tankeray Flats Estate – scenes in which Bob Cryer and community copper Ron Smollett had been attacked by rampaging youths – 17-year-old Martin Grant was found stabbed on the mostly owner-occupied Cresswell Court Estate. Grant had been the chief suspect in a burglary and assault case six months earlier but the Crown Prosecution Service had dropped the case through insufficient evidence. Carver felt that the attack on Grant was poetic justice but Meadows angrily reminded him that the job of CID was to uphold the law equally without fear or favour. He would not tolerate vigilantes taking matters into their own hands. Even with Brownlow demanding an explanation for the rising crime figures on the estate, Meadows was determined to do it his way and left the residents in no doubt that those who attacked Grant would be brought to justice and charged with conspiracy to murder.

SUN HILL – *The Facts*

Before playing DC Liz Rawton, actress Libby Davison had appeared on **The Bill** *as a prostitute.*

>5 January 1993
The Bill goes thrice weekly

>26 March 1993
DC Viv Martella is shot dead by building society robbers

>15 May 1993
Ted Roach resigns after punching Inspector Andrew Monroe in the face

Viv Martella makes the fatal mistake of quizzing a gang of armed robbers.

The Death of Viv Martella

Whereas Mike Dashwood had left Sun Hill in high spirits, Viv Martella departed in a body bag. Late for a briefing, she was deliberately excluded by Burnside from an operation to nail a gang of armed robbers in the act. Hurt by the snub, she decided to help Stamp with a routine investigation into a handbag-snatcher, only to stumble unwittingly across the raiders' car. Unaware that the men were carrying guns, she approached the vehicle and was promptly shot dead by one of the occupants. Burnside was in an unforgiving mood. When he described Martella as a 'silly bitch', Carver took a swing at him and berated him for a lack of compassion. Unrepentant, Burnside told Meadows that he refused to feel responsible for her death and put on a show of false grief. Nevertheless it was he who took on the thankless task of clearing out Martella's personal possessions from her desk.

The End of Roach

Next to go – and in almost equally acrimonious circumstances – was Ted Roach. When Stamp and Quinnan were called to deal with a fight in a pub, they found to their dismay (but probably not their surprise) that one of

>7 September 1993
DI Frank Burnside leaves Sun Hill on special duties

>2 August 1994
Chris Deakin's first day as a DS at Sun Hill

>9 September 1994
DI Sally Johnson is charged with manslaughter

Sally Johnson supervises the ill-fated raid.

the combatants was Roach. Even by Ted's standards he was in a bad way and he did little to improve his prospects by proceeding to punch Inspector Monroe in the face. Although they'd had a few run-ins down the years, Burnside did his utmost to prevent Roach from losing his job. He coerced Roach's adversary in the pub not to press charges and managed to sweet-talk Monroe into giving Ted another chance. All it needed, Burnside told Roach, was an apology to Monroe. But Ted, more bullish than usual, ignored Burnside's conciliatory efforts and resigned. As Meadows caustically remarked, it was the end of an era...not just for Roach, but also for Burnside.

Criticised for his persistent failure to supervise Roach and with Meadows breathing down his neck all the time, Burnside decided it was time to move on, announcing that he had been assigned to special secret duties on orders from above. Frank always did like to keep them guessing.

The Trial of DI Johnson

Burnside's replacement was the fiercely ambitious Sally Johnson from Stafford Row. She set about antagonising most of the Relief by her disdainful attitude. June Ackland, in particular, longed for the chance to see her fall flat on her face. She did not have long to wait. Johnson's raid on a flat on the Cockcroft Estate went horribly wrong when a young boy fell from a third-floor balcony while trying to

make his escape. Worse was to follow. Investigating the ownership of a sawn-off shotgun found in a house fire, Lines was led to crack dealer Lee Ruddick, who also acted as pimp for Claudia Morris, a prostitute who was badly burned in the blaze. Acting on information supplied by Claudia, Johnson planned a raid on Ruddick's crack den but when confronted, Ruddick shoved a lump of crack into his mouth. Johnson desperately

>27 January 1995
Sally Johnson is elbowed out of Sun Hill

>3 February 1995
DS Don Beech arrives at Sun Hill

>3 March 1995
Chief Insp. Philip Cato resigns

Johnson faces the music in the witness box.

out by the book, the Complaints Investigation Bureau (CIB) were called in, and when Claudia blamed Johnson for Ruddick's death, the DI was facing a manslaughter charge. Meadows was unimpressed by Johnson's version of events and asked her pointedly whether her attempt to remove the crack from Ruddick's mouth was an attempt to save his life or merely to gather evidence. Her reply was non-committal. CIB pointed out how suspicious it was that none of the other officers on the raid had witnessed the fateful moment when the deceased banged his head. Meadows managed to lean on Claudia and persuade her to drop all charges but just when Johnson thought she was in the clear, she learned that Ruddick's family were going to bring a private prosecution against her.

tried to remove the foaming crack but in the struggle Ruddick fell, hitting his head on a bedside cabinet. He died in St Hugh's from compression of the brain, probably caused by the blow to the head.

Johnson was in big trouble. Although she assured Brownlow that the raid was carried

With Johnson's trial hanging over her, Sun Hill was plunged into further controversy when a prisoner died in custody. CID had mounted an operation to monitor notorious bullion robber Kenny Stone as he bought a large consignment of cocaine but they failed to catch him in possession. While Meadows tried to scrape

>**12 October 1995**
DS Jo Morgan gunned down outside Sun Hill station

>**19 January 1996**
PC Cathy Marshall drowns while chasing a suspect

>**22 March 1996**
The Bill celebrates its 1,000[th] episode – 'Blood Brothers'

Matt Boyden and Philip Cato read the riot act to Sgt. Ray Steele (left).

together sufficient evidence to charge him, Stone was thrown into the cells on a particularly rowdy night. With the cell buzzers going constantly, Custody Sgt. Ray Steele decided to turn them off for five minutes' respite, but when officers looked in on Stone in order to release him on bail, they found him lying dead on the floor. The inquest was a messy business. The Stone family alleged false imprisonment, malicious prosecution and negligence on the part of the police, and when medical evidence revealed that Stone had suffered two heart attacks in the cell – the second being fatal – the dead man's relatives called Steele a murderer for having switched off the buzzers. To the relief of all at Sun Hill, the verdict was that Stone had died of natural causes, but Steele didn't escape a stern reprimand from Monroe over his reckless actions.

At Johnson's trial Claudia changed her tune

SUN HILL – *The Facts*

Shaun Scott (DI Chris Deakin) played several villains in early episodes of **The Bill,** *ranging from a seedy landlord to a dodgy gym instructor.*

>18 September 1996
June Ackland passes her sergeants' exam

>28 November 1997
June Ackland is suspended from duty, accused of conspiracy to handle stolen money

>12 December 1997
Probationer Luke Ashton's mum turns up to watch him on traffic duty during his first day at Sun Hill

Cato's disciplinarian approach ruffled even Derek Conway's feathers.

again, claiming that Meadows had bullied her into withdrawing her complaint, threatening that unless she did so she would get life for drug trafficking. When the tape of their conversation was played back, Meadows came over as distinctly menacing. It began to look as though more than one member of the Sun Hill hierarchy was on trial. Facing accusations that she had deliberately banged Ruddick's head on the cabinet, Johnson proved an evasive, unconvincing witness. The prosecution smelled a cover-up but, after originally failing to reach a decision, the jury found Johnson not guilty. On their way out of court, Meadows said he expected that would be the last time Johnson would ever try and save a crackhead – a sentiment with which she agreed, replying tartly, 'Good riddance!'

Boyden's Brawl

If charm were taxed, Chief Inspector Philip Cato would qualify for a rebate. His transfer from Barton Street was greeted with barely disguised disgust by the rank and file of Sun Hill, who still blamed him for the downfall of Tom Penny. Cato's strict disciplinarian approach did nothing to suggest he had been misjudged. By contrast Matt Boyden, the new sergeant, possessed a tongue that was as smooth as Cato's head. Boyden always had an eye for the main chance, particularly if it was wearing a short skirt, but his womanising ways soon landed him in hot water at Sun Hill. One night PC George Garfield was taken to hospital after being beaten up by a burglar. Everyone on the relief was puzzled why Boyden, who was on duty just a street away from where Garfield was

Ackland realises to her horror that her home is about to go up in flames.

attacked, had not gone to his aid. Boyden claimed that his radio was down but it transpired that the real reason he had failed to respond to Garfield's call for immediate assistance was because he was busy having sex with CID snout Jackie Welland. After being hauled over the coals by Monroe, Boyden found his locker filled with white feathers. On Garfield's return to duty, the relief placed bets on the likelihood of him punching Boyden. Cryer tried to keep them apart but Garfield would not be denied his moment of satisfaction. To Boyden's credit, he refrained from fighting back or putting Garfield on a charge.

Terror For Ackland

June Ackland always tried to rise above petty squabbles such as the Boyden/Garfield incident; anyway she had more important things to worry about when someone took a shot at her in the street, killing an innocent onlooker by mistake. Then a few days later petrol was poured through her letterbox and set alight. June was put in a safe house and told

Ackland received little support from Brownlow when under investigation from CIB.

SUN HILL – *The Facts*

Before becoming an actor, Shaun Scott (DI Chris Deakin) went for an interview with Surrey Police.

to draw up a list of people who might hold a grudge against her. She came up with 23 possibles but one by one they were eliminated, leaving June to conclude that the only way to flush out her would-be assassin was to go back out on the streets and act as bait. With former Sun Hill DS Jo Morgan working on the case for Regional Crime Squad, CID were tipped off about Micky Sieger, an ex-squaddie who had been mouthing off about 'doing a copper'. The name meant nothing to Ackland until Sieger's ex-girlfriend revealed that he hated the police for fitting up his friend, Carl Mitchell. Mitchell's name was on Ackland's list until CID discovered that he had killed himself in

Shadwell Prison. Now, it emerged, Mitchell's mother, Mrs Cooper, had hired Sieger to kill Ackland as revenge for her son's death. Under interrogation Mrs Cooper pretended that Sieger was waiting for Ackland at the safe house. Plans were made for Ackland to go there and flush him out but Morgan eventually forced Mrs Cooper to admit that she was lying. As Morgan ran to the front of Sun Hill to prevent Ackland and armed officers leaving by car, Sieger drew up on a motorcycle and fired a hail of bullets at the windscreen. Ackland escaped unharmed but her relief was short-lived when she saw that Morgan had been shot dead.

June was in further strife a year after her elevation to sergeant. A long-standing snout, Cherry Towner, arranged to meet her in order to repay £250 that June had once lent her, but the notes were found to be part of the proceeds of an armed robbery carried out by Cherry's husband Roy some years earlier. He had done time for the robbery but the cash had never been recovered. With CIB hot on the case, Ackland had to admit that the loan had not been logged because it was a personal matter, to pay off a fine, and that she had met Cherry alone, contrary to regulations, as it was a last-minute arrangement and the station was short-staffed. Ackland was charged with conspiracy to handle stolen money and suspended from duty. With June's job on the line, Cherry was traced to St. Hugh's, where she was horrified to hear of the trouble she had caused. She hadn't known that the money was 'hot' and exonerated June from involvement in anything underhand. Grateful for Bob Cryer's support throughout her ordeal, June offered to help him with his paperwork. He suggested she buy him a drink instead.

Sally Johnson's career never recovered from the manslaughter charge and she was shunted off to a desk job. Her successor, Chris Deakin, was just one of a number of new faces in CID – including Suzi Croft, Liz Rawton, Rod Skase, Geoff Daly, John Boulton and Don Beech. Some would leave a more lasting mark than others. Internal divisions and personality clashes sparked enough electricity to crash the National Grid but one occasion on which everyone pulled together was the Sun Hill Christmas production of *Aladdin*. The drama was by no means confined to the stage when the brother of a man on trial for assault crept into the theatre with the intention of silencing Deakin before he could give evidence in court the following day. The culprit was eventually apprehended by the irate director, Polly Page, assisted by Hollis and Garfield…in the guise of a pantomime cow. It wasn't one to shout about on B wing at Strangeways.

One of the new faces at Sun Hill, John Boulton joined Jim Carver and Frank Burnside in CID.

GRAHAM COLE

Graham Cole knows exactly what he likes best about being in *The Bill* – the driving stunts. But there was one time when he momentarily feared his worst nightmare had come true: he thought he had killed the director!

'We were at Battersea Power Station doing a long, complicated driving sequence,' recalls Graham, 'and I had to come flying up the road and stop on a very precise mark. It was difficult to do because the land there is bumpy. Anyway I was revving the car up ready to go and just as I heard "Action", the director walked in front of it. I hit the brakes but he disappeared. And I thought, "I've killed him!" I got out of the car and found that he was OK – he'd run out of the way just in time. But I went mad with him because it was really scary. Apart from anything else, how would you write out the accident report? Of course, this was several years ago, and they're much more careful now!'

Although he trained as an orthopaedic technician, Graham had always dreamed of becoming an actor. 'I'd pay 6d to go to Saturday morning cinema when I was eight and watch John Wayne or Humphrey Bogart. I wanted to

INTERVIEW

be those guys. My wife Cherry will tell you that even now if I'm hoovering I'm not in the real world – I'm finding dust on Tutankhamen's tomb!'

Father-of-two Graham did 15 years in repertory and musicals before joining *The Bill*. 'I only appeared unnamed in background scenes at first, but I made a point of always doing something wrong – chewing gum or putting my feet up on the desk. That got me noticed.

'I'm quite fond of Tony Stamp and if I ever had to call 999, I would hope that it would be someone like him who would come out. At least he looks as if he's going to do something. I try to portray the world-weariness of the

Stamp is never afraid to get involved in the rough stuff.

as PC Tony Stamp

knife attacks and being battered with baseball bats while conveying the thrill of answering a call in Sierra One, like John Wayne riding his horse into God knows what. I still make a point of going out with the police a couple of times a year just so that I can stay on the ball and keep up to date with new procedures. I must be doing OK because I often notice when I'm out driving with Cherry that the public quickly put on their seat belts if they pull alongside me at traffic lights!'

Last year Stamp suffered the trauma of being wrongly accused of

child abuse. Many actors would have shied away from such a storyline but Graham relished the opportunity. 'I was very excited about doing that story because I knew what it would mean to Stamp, to be isolated from his colleagues. And it was great to be able to spread it over a period of time rather than have it all done and dusted in an hour like the old days. I spent 12 weeks working on that and it did get to me. Driving home, I'd have to pull into a lay-by and have a bit of a cry to get rid of my emotions and compose myself before meeting my family.

And I got hundreds of letters of support from people saying they knew Stamp was innocent.

'The other tough one was when I ran over a guy in Sierra One. The Met. were really helpful and allowed me to talk to officers who had been in a similar position. But I managed to put that storyline to good use. Earlier I'd had a bet with the Flying Squad who said they'd give £100 to my favourite charity if I could get the Flying Squad tie on TV. Stamp nearly always wears a uniform so it wasn't easy and it took me over a year to work it in. But when he went to court on the dangerous driving charge I wore the tie. Afterwards they sent me a cheque and a note with 'You Bastard' written across the top.'

BAD BOYS INC.

PC Eddie Santini

Eddie Santini reckoned he could pull a woman faster than the barmaid at his local could pull a pint. His smouldering Latin looks and smooth chat-up lines sent many a Sun Hill heart aflutter. Even unimpressionable girls like Polly Page admitted he was a welcome addition to the ranks. That was the thing about Eddie – he seemed a nice guy, until you got to know him. One or two of the lads had him sussed from the start. Dave Quinnan didn't rate him, if only because Eddie was encroaching upon his territory, threatening his status as the station's most eligible bachelor. It was combs at dawn.

Above all Santini liked a challenge. Easy girls were ten a penny in his line of work but he relished the prospect of going where few men had gone before, of tackling rarely conquered peaks. Rosie Fox was his Everest. An attractive brunette, PC Fox was on attachment to Sun Hill and, at the suggestion of Liz Rawton, was paired with Santini to investigate the death of a young junkie whose body had been found washed up on the banks of the Thames. Both were forceful and opinionated, with the result that the atmosphere between them was heated rather than warm. But Santini wanted her and after they had been goaded into sharing a drunken kiss at the post-case celebration, he pinned her down in the locker room, ignoring her pleas to stop. It was only when he was momentarily distracted by a

Eddie Santini pushes things too far with Rosie Fox.

>**9 January 1998**
The famous feet are dropped from the titles of *The Bill*. The first episode without them is titled 'Villain'

>**2 May 1998**
The death of actor Kevin Lloyd, who played DC 'Tosh' Lines

>**8 May 1998**
PC Mike Jarvis leaves to join the Diplomatic Protection Group

Dave Quinnan remained resolutely impervious to Santini's charm.

noise that he finally pulled away.

Refusing to believe that she could resist his charms, Santini continued to go Fox hunting. He turned up on her doorstep with wine and flowers while at work he used every opportunity to harass her verbally and physically. When he again overstepped the mark at a charity paintball game, Fox asked Ackland not to pair them together in future. Ackland was unsympathetic and told her to sort herself out. Following weeks of anguish, Fox decided to make an allegation of sexual

assault against Santini, but it left her virtually friendless in the station. She was branded neurotic and a liar. When Meadows said there was insufficient evidence to proceed, Fox realised the only way out of her

SUN HILL – *The Facts*

Daniel MacPherson (PC Cameron Tait) was voted Most Dateable Guy in Australia for 1998. He is also a champion triathlete in his native country.

>28 July 1998
DS Alistair Greig quits Sun Hill

>27 August 1998
Format reverts to one-hour

>27 October 1998
Detectives John Boulton and Jim Carver meet up with Frank Burnside in Manchester

nightmare was to seek a transfer.

Even with Fox gone, Santini continued to paint her as mentally unhinged. Just about the only person not taken in by his spin was Quinnan, who discovered that this wasn't the first time that Santini had been accused of harassment. Soon others began to have their suspicions, notably Bob Cryer, who had Santini down as a slippery customer with a serious attitude problem. Feisty PC Vicky Hagen had

Santini convinces Vicky Hagen of his sincerity.

no such doubts and was only too happy to help Santini christen the bed he was having delivered to his new flat. She became Eddie's number one cheerleader.

The life of a humble PC wasn't glamorous enough for Santini. He longed for more excitement – a job with more kudos — and set his sights on a move to the Drugs Squad. To this end, he arranged a meeting with Timpney,

a DS in the Drugs Squad, who told him he'd need to come up with quality information on major operators if he wanted to join the team. So when Jess Orton, co-owner of the High Hat drinking club and one of Santini's casual lovers, mentioned that her ex, John Ferguson, was a big league drug fixer who wanted to launder money through her club, Santini jumped at the chance of becoming involved. Neglecting his regular duties at Sun Hill, Santini, posing as Jess's current husband Steve, attended a rendezvous with Ferguson and Jess, where he was handed a brown envelope containing £6,000 in return for agreeing to the money laundering deal. Under pressure from Timpney, Santini became suspicious about Jess's relationship with Ferguson. Sneaking off patrol, he confronted Jess outside her club moments before a huge explosion destroyed the place. When it became apparent that an accelerant had been used, AMIP were called in. Among their investigating officers was Santini's arch enemy, Rosie – now Sergeant – Fox.

Whilst managing to stay one step ahead of the law with a little help from Hagen, Santini couldn't outsmart Ferguson, who, having uncovered Santini's true identity, had him kidnapped and beaten up. Santini realised that Ferguson had torched the club in an attempt to silence those who had tried to stitch him

>**2 March 1999**
  Dave Quinnan almost dies after being stabbed

>**11 May 1999**
  Jim Carver goes back into Uniform while DC Danny Glaze is his replacement in CID

>**14 October 1999**
  Broken-hearted George Garfield leaves Sun Hill

up. He was clearly a dangerous man to know. For the first time in his life Santini began to feel out of his depth but, still eager to join the Drugs Squad, he passed on to Timpney the names of Ferguson and his boss, Sherman.

Convinced that Santini was heavily involved, Fox encouraged Jess to implicate him, and when Jess declined, Fox controversially released her on bail. Santini was waiting for Jess on her return home. They argued bitterly at the top of the stairs and Jess fell to her death, Santini managed to escape over the back fence just as the police kicked in the front door. Visibly scratched on his neck from the struggle, he dashed back to his flat…and the welcoming arms of Hagen.

Rosie Fox did not give up until she'd got her man.

>16 December 1999
PC Dave Quinnan gets married

>17 February 2000
DC Rod Skase leaves Sun Hill before he can be pushed

>2 April 2000
PC Eddie Santini is shot dead in his flat

Santini's relief at being acquitted was short-lived.

6 July 2000
First episode in a six-part spin-off, *Burnside*

>26 September 2000
Former DS Ted Roach returns in a two-parter

>17 October 2000
DS John Boulton is murdered by DS Don Beech

Although taken off the case over her failure to protect Jess, Fox refused to be deflected from her pursuit of Santini. However, he appeared to have covered his tracks until Hagen discovered a pair of house keys under his pillow. And when Fox mentioned to Hagen that Jess's killer must have had the keys to her house in order to gain entry, Hagen's self-delusion finally collapsed. The keys, the scratch, they all made sense. Fox had got her man.

A number of important people were worried about Santini spilling the beans in court, among them Ferguson and Sherman. On the night before the trial, one of Sherman's heavies murdered Fox in her hotel bath, making it look like suicide. After arranging for Ferguson to be disposed of, Sherman turned his attentions to Timpney, who was supposed to be providing Santini with an alibi for the time of Jess Orton's murder. In the witness box the next day Timpney blew Santini's alibi. Santini knew he had been got at.

Yet the jury returned a verdict of 'not guilty'. Santini rushed home to find Timpney waiting gun in hand. 'It's you or me – that's the deal,' said Timpney before coolly shooting him dead. Eddie Santini never did make the Drugs Squad.

Stamp Kills a Pedestrian

Dependable Tony Stamp was just about the least likely person at Sun Hill to find himself on the receiving end of criminal charges, but beneath that teddy bear façade lurked a competitively macho streak. It came to the surface when Reg Hollis, with his uncanny knack of getting under people's skin, implied that Vicky Hagen was a faster Area Car driver

Stamp lays flowers at Simon Attwell's grave.

than Stamp. To be considered second best to any driver would have been an affront to Stamp's pride, but to suggest that he was inferior to a woman was simply too much to take. So when an urgent call came through to assist Polly Page, Stamp responded immediately, determined to be first on the scene, only to find his attempt at a short cut down a narrow one-way street barred by a large van. Reversing frantically, he ploughed into a pedestrian, Simon Attwell, who later died in hospital.

Stamp was a broken man. As rumours spread that he had been racing Hagen to the scene, he was suspended from the wheel and charged with causing death by dangerous

The streets of Sun Hill are no place for the faint-hearted.

driving. He tried to pay his respects at the funeral but Attwell's girlfriend took exception and reported him to Inspector Monroe for harassment. With Quinnan (who was a passenger in the car) as a reluctant witness for the prosecution, Stamp was facing a sentence of up to ten years but, to his immense relief, he

SUN HILL – *The Facts*

Prince William has admitted that he enjoys The Bill and June Ackland is his favourite.

was found not guilty. However, he was fined for driving without due care and attention and ordered to appear before a police disciplinary board. The internal hearing represented another traumatic day for Stamp who, losing his nerve at the prospect of losing his job, walked out at one point and was only persuaded to return by Federation Rep. George Garfield. It was a wise decision: Stamp was reinstated. It would be the last time he would try to compete with a fast mover like Vicky Hagen.

Quinnan comes under attack from a gang of youths. He was lucky to escape with his life.

Quinnan in Peril

DS John Boulton was about as popular with Uniform as an overtime ban. Unpleasant, unprofessional and uncaring, the new recruit from Barton Street had a habit of making enemies wherever he went. He trod on more toes than Tony Stamp at the Christmas disco. Adopting the principles of Machiavelli rather than Sir Robert Peel, Boulton would stop at nothing to get a result, even if it meant putting other people's lives in danger…as Dave Quinnan would testify only too well.

Boulton was hot on the trail of a pair of sadistic burglars who doused pensioners in petrol and threatened to set them alight before ransacking their homes. When the name of Mick Glover came up as a possible suspect, Boulton decided to raid his flat even though the move might jeopardise Quinnan and Garfield's six-week observation of the premises and put their informant, Janie, at risk. Ignoring their concerns, Boulton pressed ahead but found absolutely nothing. Angry and frustrated, he consoled himself with bringing in Glover on a trumped-up charge of assault. As

SUN HILL – *The Facts*

The officers' gleaming white shirts are washed with a black sock at first so that there isn't too much glare on the screen. Around 60 are washed and ironed every day.

Garfield reacts angrily to Boulton's jibes over the stabbing of Quinnan.

Quinnan and Garfield had feared, Janie was immediately targeted as a 'grass' and on answering an emergency call-out to her flat, they found it trashed and daubed in graffiti. While Garfield remained in the flat, Quinnan chased a young suspect, Kevin White, into the nearby youth centre and managed to grab him. Suddenly a gang of teenagers emerged from hiding and launched a vicious, sustained attack on Quinnan. Hearing his colleague's desperate pleas for assistance, Garfield raced to the scene but was unable to gain entry to the centre and could only look on helplessly as

Quinnan took a savage beating. Unconscious and in danger of bleeding to death from a stab wound, Quinnan was rushed to St. Hugh's and only pulled through following an emergency operation.

White was eventually charged with the knifing but the bad feeling persisted between Garfield and Boulton, the latter claiming that Quinnan had only himself to blame for not wearing a stab vest. When Boulton further riled Garfield by asking him whether he felt guilty about letting his mate get stabbed, George exploded with anger and had to be dragged off a quivering Boulton by Sgt. Boyden. Boulton was now public enemy number one around Sun Hill. He continued to defend his actions but June Ackland put him in his place by telling him that nobody trusted him any more. The animosity between Garfield and Boulton showed no signs of abating, and when Boulton goaded him again about Quinnan, Garfield responded with a head-butt. As Boulton walked quietly away, burly DC Duncan Lennox admitted that he would have head-butted Boulton himself if Garfield hadn't done it.

Carry on Nurse

Quinnan was making steady progress from his injuries, aided by the care and attention he was receiving from nurse Jenny Delaney. Among his many visitors was Boulton, who arrived with flowers and an apology. Garfield was another frequent caller, but was really more interested in seeing Jenny than Quinnan. Eventually he plucked up the courage to ask her out for a drink. What's more, she said yes! It was enough to have given Quinnan a relapse.

Garfield was habitually unlucky in love but hoped that Jenny would be his Esmerelda. Although she liked him, she couldn't help notice that his animal magnetism was equal to that of an eager-to-please puppy. Quinnan, on the other hand, exuded sex appeal and danger. He and Jenny began exchanging meaningful glances; there was a definite chemistry between them. Garfield was so blissfully happy that he remained oblivious to what was going on around him until, while waiting for an answer to his marriage proposal, he caught Jenny and Quinnan in a passionate embrace.

Nurse Jenny Delaney puts a smile back on Quinnan's face.

That was his answer.

Hurt and angered by his friend's betrayal, Garfield lunged at Quinnan back at the Section House before embarking on a heavy drinking session at The Canley Arms. He then staggered around to Jenny's flat, only to be apprehended by the police for creating a disturbance in the street outside. In the melee, he punched one of the officers in the face and was arrested but, after much pulling of strings, he was freed without charge. Later Quinnan tried to smooth the troubled waters, only for Garfield to take another swing at him whereupon a furious Monroe gave the pair a dressing down with orders to sort it out before the end of the shift. Quinnan offered to put in for a transfer but Boyden, who had first-hand experience of Garfield's temper, advised George to reconsider *his* position before he did himself or someone else an injury. Garfield took the hint and told Quinnan not to put in for a transfer. As the pair reached an uneasy truce, Garfield announced that he would be leaving Sun Hill instead.

Having got the girl, Quinnan wasted no time in proposing. During a hectic stag night, he sought sanctuary at Polly Page's flat, where she suddenly blurted out her true feelings for him. Quinnan had had no idea how Polly felt and confessed that he saw her merely as a good mate. The next day Polly told him to forget everything she had said – for both their sakes. To add to Polly's depression, Stamp suggested they go to the wedding together since neither of them had partners. Outside

The secret policemen's brawl: Garfield wades into Quinnan over his relationship with Jenny.

the registry office Stamp spotted a wanted burglar and, realising that they would be late for the wedding if they drove him back to Sun Hill, decided to take him into the ceremony. When Garfield turned up unexpectedly halfway through, it wasn't only the cake you could have cut with a knife and there were further problems when best man Hollis (who had assumed the role after Stamp declared himself unavailable) announced that the police photographer he had hired to do the pictures had to leave in order to photograph a dead body. Then, just as the party was about to get into full swing on the reception boat, Polly had to talk a suicidal woman out of jumping from a bridge and Carver dived into the river to rescue a relative of Jenny's who had fallen into the water. All in all, it was definitely a day to remember.

Carver Hits the Bottle

To say 'Sunny' Jim Carver was happy in CID would be a gross exaggeration because he was never happy anywhere. He always looked as if he had the weight of several worlds on his shoulders. However, he did find detective work fulfilling and so it came as a devastating blow when he faced returning to Uniform as part of the Tenure scheme. Despite words of encouragement from old friends like June Ackland, who reminded him of his early days at Sun Hill and how he had always wanted to stay in Uniform, he feared it would be a question of making the most of a bad job. He struggled to adjust to the switch, often ploughing a detective's lone furrow and forgetting that he was now supposed to be a team player. He was bored by the periods of inactivity. He was used to acting on hunches not sitting on haunches.

Feeling isolated from the rest of the relief and embittered by a run-in with Deakin, he considered taking a job as a security manager but was rejected for his 'defensive' attitude. As he started to drown his sorrows in drink, he became increasingly belligerent, even lashing out at Reg Hollis — the equivalent of kicking Mother Theresa in the shins.

If nothing else, Carver had always been reliable but, with his grip on reality more tenuous by the day, his work

Three's a crowd.

Skase maintains a watching brief while Carver comes up with a collar.

deteriorated alarmingly. Due to give evidence at an important trial, he arrived in court late, drunk and dishevelled, and when he did make it into the witness box his rambling, incoherent testimony totally contradicted DC Rod Skase's version of events. A furious Meadows reported Carver's behaviour to Monroe, who, aware of Carver's drink problem, decided to get him away from the station for a while by sending him out with Stamp to guard a consignment of seized drugs on their route from the Area warehouse to an incinerator. It was not a wise move. Sharing a bottle with a warehouseman,

Carver let slip details of the next delivery. The following morning as the convoy pulled out of the warehouse with Stamp and Carver behind, Carver complained of a dodgy stomach and insisted that Stamp pull over. Stamp refused to risk it, at which point Carver opened the door of the moving car, forcing Stamp to swerve to a halt. Once Carver had been violently sick in some bushes, Stamp put his foot down and caught up with the convoy, only to discover that, in their absence, the drugs van had been ambushed and an Armed Response officer shot. Finding Carver's sudden illness all too convenient, Stamp wondered whether he had tipped off the gunmen. At best, Carver had become a liability.

Just when he probably thought things couldn't get any worse, Carver bumped into a fellow drunk called Johnjo, who invited him back to his flat on the Larkmead Estate and proceeded to offer him the services of his wife, Claire. Carver initially declined because he wanted to sleep off his hangover but that evening he and Claire started to chat about their shared descent into alcoholism. The following morning he woke up semi-naked in Claire's bed. To his horror, she was lying dead next to him, his tie around her neck like a tourniquet. When Sun Hill officers arrived, they

SUN HILL – *The Facts*

Natalie Roles, who plays DS Debbie McAllister, had previously been seen on **The Bill** *as a cat burglar's accomplice.*

found Carver's warrant card next to the body.

With the hunt on for the missing Carver, Johnjo's corpse was discovered in a nearby rubbish chute. He was wearing Carver's suit and had been stabbed. Frank Burnside, Carver's old boss and now a DCI, was brought in to lead the inquiry. Not renowned for being sympathetic to suspects, whom he invariably referred to as 'you slag', Burnside made an exception in Carver's case and it was with

Smith and Klein wait as Carver is called to the bar.

Friends reunited. Burnside lays down the law to Carver about his drinking.

serious misgivings that, after tracking him down to a hostel, he arrested Carver on suspicion of murder. Carver admitted to having blackouts and said that he couldn't be certain whether or not he had killed Claire. But just as it was looking grim for Jim, the real killer was apprehended – Johnjo and Claire's lodger, Chris Riley, who had strangled Claire in a jealous rage after seeing her asleep next to Carver, before murdering Johnjo during an argument. Despite Carver's innocence being established, Brownlow wanted to sack him, but

he was talked round by Conway and Monroe. Brownlow reluctantly agreed to a stay of execution on condition that Carver spent at least the next two weeks drying out at the police nursing home. For Jim Carver, it was the last chance saloon.

Desperate Don

Burnside became a frequent visitor to Sun Hill during this period – too frequent for some people's liking. Meadows, who preferred to play things by the book, called him a

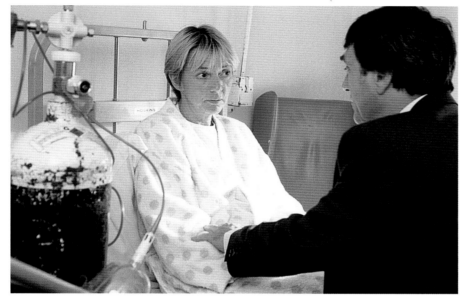

The caring face of
Don Beech.

'chancer' and warned Boulton against getting too involved with Burnside, saying that he'd lead him down the sewer. But as Meadows would later discover to his cost, when it came to corruption he should have been focussing a lot closer to home – on one of his own Detective Sergeants, Don Beech.

Beech didn't just bend the rules, he broke them into little pieces. He was on the payroll of a number of major London villains who, from time to time, would call him in for a favour. If it could be done without endangering his position in the force, he would set the wheels in motion – in return for a fat brown envelope full of readies. He had his finger in more pies than Little Jack Horner. He accepted a bung of £20,000 to swing a trial; he took a bribe of £10,000 in a money laundering case; and, while breaking into a suspect's flat to recover vital evidence, he attacked Burnside when the latter arrived unexpectedly. Of course, none of this had ever been proved. Beech was far too clever for that. And when he was literally caught with his trousers down in the company of a prostitute by PC Debbie Keane, he managed to talk his way out of trouble. He was also in debt to the bookies – a sackable offence in the police – and had been beaten up for

Deakin failed to monitor Beech's activities.

Geoff Daly vowed to nail Beech.

sleeping with another man's wife, yet he had always come up smelling, if not exactly of roses then not of manure. Indeed in October 1998 he went to Hendon to collect his Long Service and Good Conduct award.

Among those who believed that Beech led a charmed life was his fellow DS, Geoff Daly, who was as straight as they come. Daly couldn't abide Beech's dodgy methods and was convinced that Beech was bent. When he told him so to his face, Beech pushed him in the canal. Once again Don Beech had come out on top.

Beech Turns Killer

Beech and John Boulton could have been two of a kind. Both hated Daly, whom they regarded as unbearably self-righteous, and both were prepared to tear up the rule book if necessary. The difference was that Boulton would only do so in order to nick a villain. No way was he bent. Perhaps he had more in common with Daly than he realised.

Then in 1999 another name entered the equation. On the face of it Claire Stanton was simply a new DS at Sun Hill but in reality she was a CIB 'mole' sent to spy on Beech, whose catalogue of misdemeanours had finally aroused suspicion high up. Naturally, Stanton's true identity remained a secret to all but her CIB boss, Hodges. Stanton soon found herself performing a juggling act, trying to keep tabs on Beech on the one hand and falling for Boulton on the other. A romance with Boulton was definitely not part of her brief and the distraction seriously threatened to jeopardise her investigation. Her paranoia about their liaison being exposed reached crisis point when Boulton booked them into a hotel for the night, only for the place soon to be swarming with Sun Hill officers called out to deal with an assault in one of the rooms. Leading the inquiry, Beech uncovered Stanton's secret love but kept it to himself…ready to use one day if ever he needed a favour in return. That was how Beech liked to operate.

Away from prying eyes, Beech continued to wheel and deal. During a game of poker he was introduced to Howard Fallon, a big-time villain on a recruitment drive. Fallon was mourning the hijacking of a lorry load of mobile phones (cover for a consignment of heroin) and asked Beech to help retrieve the haul before Customs became involved. By staying one step ahead of Daly's investigation, Beech succeeded in handing the drugs to Fallon and the phones to CID. Everybody was happy…except Daly, who fumed while Beech took all the plaudits for cracking the case.

Fallon was so impressed by Beech that he decided to put him on the payroll. Beech's first job for his new employer involved Rachel Booker, a lap dancer from the Starlight Club, who had been badly beaten up the previous night. Since Rachel was part of Fallon's money-laundering operation, he paid Beech £7,500 to remove incriminating papers from her flat, a task made all the more urgent by the news that written in her diary was Beech's mobile phone number. Rachel's death turned the investigation into a murder inquiry and Beech succeeded in framing her neighbour, Warren Askew. When a devastated Askew hanged himself in his cell, it was case closed as far as Beech was concerned. He phoned Fallon and told him everything was sorted.

Stanton wasn't willing to give up yet. Boulton had acquired Rachel's diary and, on phoning a number marked S.O.S., heard Beech's voice on the other end. The diary also contained a series of codes, which Stanton

Beech covers his tracks under interrogation from John Boulton and Claire Stanton.

The fatal rendezvous. Beech tries to strike a deal with Boulton.

deciphered as bank accounts. It dawned on her that Rachel was laundering money. Rachel's friend and fellow dancer, Lynette, offered a name for the real killer – Fallon's henchman, Ray Bazzini – and as the net closed in, Beech tried to save himself and his crooked associates by persuading Lynette to go away for her own safety. However, she returned a few days later to say that she was willing to give evidence against Bazzini. By now Boulton had started to suspect that Stanton was not quite who she claimed to be and so decided to go it alone. When Beech called late one night promising to divulge Bazzini's whereabouts, Boulton agreed to a rendezvous at a cement works where, for the first time, he became aware of the full extent of Beech's

involvement. Refusing his bribe and his plea for help, Boulton prepared to leave, but Beech couldn't allow that to happen. The two men fought, culminating in Beech repeatedly banging Boulton's head on the ground. Realising Boulton was dead, Beech dragged the body into a sandpit and ran off.

With the hunt on for Boulton's killer, Beech feared that Fallon would grass him up, so he set up a deal of his own with Hodges,

SUN HILL – *The Facts*

Nottingham-born Karl Collins (DC Ganny Glaze) played villain Everton Warwick in several episodes of The Bill before switching to the right side of the law.

Stanton leans on Beech.

offering everything he knew about Fallon and two bent coppers from Area Drugs in return for a charge of manslaughter. To Stanton's horror, Hodges agreed. On her way out of the room, she angrily knocked back Beech's chair and kicked him in the head, saying it was what Boulton would have wanted. It was justice of a kind.

Pretending to go along with the arrangement, Beech managed to double cross Hodges, Fallon and the two drugs officers – Tasker and Garrard – and escape by swimming down the Thames. The next day CIB descended on Sun Hill and suspended the whole of CID, who adjourned to the pub in an effort to come to terms with events. As rumours circulated that Beech was Boulton's murderer, Daly pointed out that he had never trusted him. Deakin said he wished he had never trusted him either. As Beech's immediate boss, Deakin reckoned he would be the most senior casualty in the fallout, but that doubtful honour was reserved for Brownlow who,

under pressure from Chief Superintendent Guy Mannion, a man with whom he had rarely seen eye-to-eye, announced to an astonished Uniform crew that he had resigned.

Although the CIB investigation could find no evidence that Beech had involved any other Sun Hill officers in the conspiracy, orders were given for Deakin and Daly to be transferred. Thanks to friends in high places, Meadows held on to his job by the skin of his teeth but was left in no doubt by Mannion or CIB that his failure to spot Beech's corruption rendered him incompetent. As for Beech, he evaded Stanton's clutches and jetted off to Australia. They were destined to meet again.

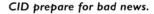

CID prepare for bad news.

LISA GEOGHAN

Whilst Polly Page seems destined to be forever unlucky in love, Lisa Geoghan has no such problems. On the contrary, she has enjoyed something of a fairytale romance with the boy she knew at school, Michael Power.

'We went to the same primary school in south-east London,' says Lisa. 'He was in the year above me and our mums used to chat at the school gates.' Lisa and Michael met again in a pub when she was 20, rekindled their friendship and in 1996 got married in Las Vegas. Then in 2002 she gave birth to their first baby, Oliver.

'Life has changed dramatically but we really wanted to have a baby. We were as ready as you can be for a life-changing experience – and he hasn't let us down, he's the icing on our cake.'

Having taken a year off, explained away by Polly's sick leave, Lisa returned to duty to find that things at Sun Hill were a little different. 'So much had changed – even the set and the layout of the studio. I needed a full induction day to get back into the swing of it! It was like getting a new job all over again and I did have

INTERVIEW

Polly Page uses her considerable charm to soothe troubled waters.

as PC Polly Page

a few first-day nerves, but soon settled down. And I was so excited to meet all the new people.'

Lisa had to miss her first day on *The Bill* because it coincided with her father's funeral. 'Dad died of a heart attack just before I joined. It was a terrible shock for the family because he was only 61, but at least he knew I had got the part. It was horrendous, but at least all my worrying about being the new girl went out of the window. I reckon that having to concentrate on playing Polly pulled me through.'

Bermondsey-born Lisa had always wanted to be an actress and studied at the famous Anna Scher Theatre School. She was offered the part of Tucker's girlfriend in *Tucker's Luck* and from that went straight into three years of the BBC series *Big Deal*. Another long-running role was that of Louise in three series of the barber's shop sitcom *Desmond's* before leaving to play chirpy Cockney Polly Page.

'I love Polly, but if she was my sister I'd have to shake her,' laughs Lisa. 'She's very dependable and loyal, a nice person to have around and real policewomen think she gives a positive image of women on the force. She really goes for what she believes in, but it's her

love life that lets her down.

'The affair with Dave Quinnan was a great storyline because Polly had always been very moral – a nice little goody two-shoes – but then she became a potential marriage-wrecker. Even the love scenes were a good laugh but a bit embarrassing because all the crew were our mates. At least because it was before the watershed, I was able to wear a flesh-coloured bikini type of thing.'

Lisa says she is puzzled by the effect Polly seems to have on male viewers. 'I often get letters asking for sexy photos, but I just send them a head shot of me in the hat. I've also had letters from the same guy asking for my old shoes. We have a right laugh about that. I don't understand why men find women in uniform sexy, but it's always "Ooh, have you got your handcuffs?" – as though you're just going to flick them out and handcuff them to the nearest railings. In their dreams!'

THE CHANDLER YEARS

Brownlow's replacement was Superintendent Tom Chandler. He was young, handsome, charismatic and energetic and as such was light years away from his predecessor. Chandler was a sparkling new Ferrari Barchetta to Brownlow's rusty old Austin Maxi. The new man impressed the vast majority of the team, especially those with long, slim legs and short skirts, while even Duncan Lennox (whose legs were neither long nor slim and who never wore a skirt to the office) had to admit that Chandler seemed 'a pretty decent bloke'.

An exception to the general euphoria was Meadows. Faced with a murder inquiry involving the son of a woman with whom he once had an affair plus a Disciplinary Board in

Tom Chandler and Des Taviner catch up on old times.

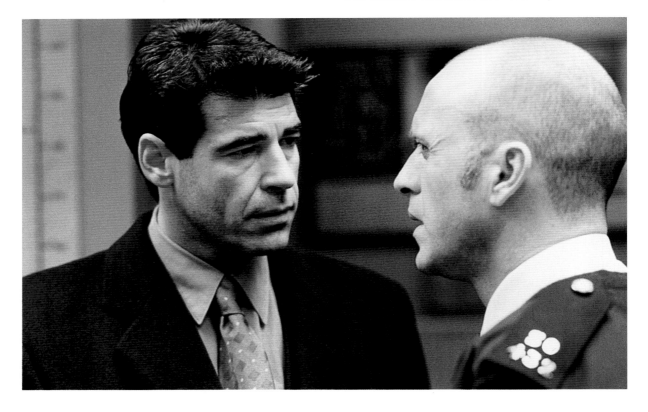

>**3 November 2000**
Sun Hill wakes up to the arrival of Superintendent Chandler and a new CID team

>**24 April 2001**
Sgt. Bob Cryer leaves Sun Hill

>**4 May 2001**
New Area Car driver Des Taviner roars into Sun Hill

Lorraine Chase helps Burnside and Lennox with their inquiries.

the wake of the Beech scandal, he also had to contend with a sustained campaign of animosity from Chandler, who clearly considered him a waste of space. Even Chandler's self-appointed yes-man, the acidic DI Alex Cullen, weighed in with his condemnation, telling Meadows that he was a liability. Although the pressure on Meadows to resign was almost unbearable, he chose to tough it out, his resolve strengthened by the possibility of skeletons in the Chandler closet. He was prepared to bide his time.

Meanwhile, Chandler's roving eye had alighted on Kate Spears who was having an on/off relationship with fellow DC, Mickey Webb. Chandler asked her to work on a series of important initiatives and began to

SUN HILL – *The Facts*

The police uniforms used in the series are genuine and are locked away for security reasons every night with no complete uniform being locked in any one cupboard.

show unnatural interest in her workload, going so far as to discuss one case over dinner. This favouritism rankled with both CID and Uniform who began taking bets on when the pair would start an affair. Hearing this, Cullen decided to act, reminding Chandler that an affair with Spears could damage his future promotion prospects. Chandler dropped her like a hot potato.

>15 June 2001
Reg Hollis is accused of murdering an elderly lady

>21 August 2001
First in six-part spin-off series, *Beech is Back*

>26 October 2001
PC Vicky Hagen seeks a transfer

Mickey Webb goes undercover to crack a gang of football hooligans.

On the Trail of a Rapist

Spears' unpopularity with the Relief was cemented when victory in an inter-station quiz earned Sun Hill a weekend away at a luxury hotel. Eager to get her claws into a local DS, Pete Cork, PC Cass Rickman seethed with jealousy when he made it clear that he preferred Spears. Spears and Cork went back to her room but things turned ugly when Spears told Cork that sex wasn't on the menu. His mood suddenly changed and, calling her a tart, he pinned her to the bed. Spears managed to fight him off and lock herself in the bathroom, only to learn the following morning that one of the female holiday reps had been attacked and murdered in the grounds. Spears wanted to reveal that Cork had tried to rape her but knew that with her reputation, nobody would believe her. Returning to Sun Hill, she was seconded to Operation Magenta, an investigation run by Liz Rawton to catch a dangerous rapist, and was horrified to learn that Cork was also joining the team.

While the rest of the team welcomed Cork's input, Spears became increasingly convinced that he was behind the attacks and began digging into his past, discovering that wherever he had worked the number of rapes in the area had increased and then dropped when he moved on. Since Rawton believed the case to be linked to a series of rapes in the East End five years earlier, Cork went to meet an old friend, DI Freddie Collins, who served on the East End rape team. Reporting back to Rawton, Cork poured cold water on the theory, saying that Collins had told him they knew who the East End rapist was – a TV repairman called

DC Kate Spears catches Chandler's roving eye.

>**3 January 2002**
Special Constable Terry Knowles is fatally stabbed in the neck

>**27 February 2002**
PC Dave Quinnan quits Sun Hill

>**28 February 2002**
The Bill adopts its new serial format

The troubled Roz Clarke has a heart-to-heart with Des Taviner.

Robert Haines. After Haines died in a fire, the rapes stopped. Now Cork came up with a plan to trap the rapist, using Polly Page, PC Roz Clarke and Spears as bait. When a man in a balaclava was arrested by Cork as he tried to attack Clarke, Cork proudly announced that they had got their man.

To Spears, it all seemed too convenient. Rawton was equally unsure, particularly after learning from an ex-DC who had worked on the East End rape case that Haines didn't fit the MO of the rapist and that the fatal fire wasn't an accident. The source added that Collins had used Haines as a smokescreen to protect someone else. Was that someone Cork?

The more digging she did, the more Rawton came to share Spears' view that Cork was somehow involved, if not as the actual rapist then as somebody who fed information to the rapist that enabled him to stay one step ahead

SUN HILL – *The Facts*

In the early days of **The Bill** *a local resident registered her protest at what she deemed to be a stereotypical portrayal of council estates as hotbeds of crime. She held up filming by stationing herself in the background with an ironing board, iron and basket full of laundry.*

>26 March 2002
Chief Inspector Derek Conway is killed by a petrol bomb

>16 April 2002
PCs Di Worrell and Ben Hayward, DC Paul Riley and Inspector Andrew Monroe are killed when a petrol bomb

is thrown at the station. PC Sam Harker and DC Kate Spears die later in hospital

of the law. Inquiries into a navy blue saloon spotted at one of the crime scenes threw up the name of Joseph Ferdinand, who had form for beating up a prostitute in 1990. Collins had handled the case. Ferdinand had last been questioned for pimping in Thames Valley but had been released without charge. The

face with Ferdinand. Realising that Collins had dropped him in it, Cork pleaded with Ferdinand to stop his reign of terror, but Ferdinand refused. A fight broke out, which ended with Ferdinand plunging a knife into Cork's chest…while Spears looked on in silent horror from her hiding place.

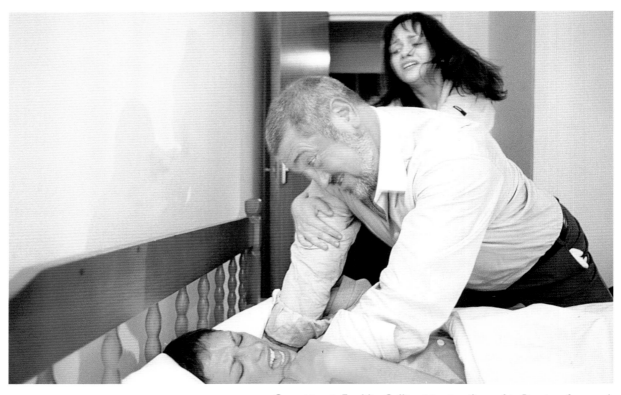

Corrupt cop Freddie Collins tries to silence Liz Rawton for good.

investigating officer on that occasion was Cork.

Cork was becoming rattled by Rawton's line of inquiry and contacted Collins to demand an urgent meeting. Acting on her own initiative, Spears followed Cork as he left his hotel and drove to a lonely warehouse where, instead of meeting Collins, he came face to

Ferdinand's car was found to contain the full rapist's kit – rope, mask, tape and gloves. The murdered holiday rep's necklace was also discovered among the trophies he kept of his victims, but there was no sign of the man himself. Now that Cork was dead, Collins set out to silence Rawton but was overpowered by

>2 May 2002
On the day of the memorial service for the victims of the bombing, DS Debbie McAllister seduces Superintendent

Chandler in the disabled toilet. DC Eva Sharpe arrives at Sun HIll

>16 May 2002
June Ackland is selected to run the new Borough Community Safety Unit

a blow to the head from Spears and forced to assist in the hunt for Ferdinand. The latter proved an elusive and deadly quarry, managing to kill Collins and kidnap Webb, Rawton and Spears. With Webb in the boot and a knife pressed to Rawton's side, Spears was ordered to drive. Noticing that Ferdinand wasn't wearing a seat belt, she distracted him with flattering conversation. When he momentarily lent forward from his seat in the back, she suddenly slammed on the brakes to send him hurtling through the windscreen. Spears had proved a point to all those who had doubted her. She just wished there had been an easier way.

McAllister and the Snout

If Kate Spears was a casualty of Chandler's philandering, few would ever choose to describe DS Debbie McAllister as a victim. Instead it was the people she encountered and manipulated who were the victims. Devious Debbie has always looked after number one, using her sexuality as a means of career advancement and making a point of never sleeping with anyone below the rank of DI. Safe sex with McAllister is when the tape recorder is switched off.

She first introduced the Sun Hill casting couch following a disastrous undercover operation that was designed to snare a drug dealer. With no evidence, she was forced to let the suspect go but took a shine to his legal representative, solicitor's clerk Jamie Ross.

Debbie McAllister: don't be fooled by the smile.

>27 June 2002
Gina Gold arrives as Sun Hill's new inspector. Ken Drummond also arrives

>2 July 2002
PC Luke Ashton returns to Sun Hill

>11 July 2002
PC Kerry Young makes her debut

Joyless DI Alex Cullen.

Acting on information gleaned from Ross over a leisurely drink, she earned much-needed Brownie points with Cullen and proposed to Ross that he become an informant on a more permanent basis. To help him make up his mind, she pointed out that he had a past record, which she could use to prevent him having access to prisoners and therefore lose him his job at the solicitors' office. Ross was happy to oblige, particularly at the prospect of McAllister paying him in kind. His reward came after he helped trap a gang of armed robbers in the act of raiding a betting shop. McAllister was very grateful. But Ross began to worry about the risks he was taking and said he wanted out, whereupon McAllister simply hung him out to dry. It was easy to see what Chandler would later see in her.

McAllister and Ross did rekindle their relationship some weeks later, when the dust had settled. The seemingly affluent Ross claimed to have a wealthy backer for a new business venture but when McAllister discovered that he was in deep with drug dealers and hit men, it was her turn to feel used. He agreed to a deal whereby he would hand her a dangerous dealer named Swain. The meeting was set up for a restaurant but Swain, having realised that Ross was a plant, kept his cards close to his chest. Fearing for Ross's safety, McAllister wanted him pulled out but Cullen decided to let it run. As Ross and Swain left the restaurant, Ross was gunned down by a professional contract killer who quickly made his escape. McAllister was left kneeling by the body, wondering whether she had played one game too many.

Quinnan's Love Triangle

Another relationship that was doomed to failure was Dave Quinnan's marriage. Jenny had set her sights on a district nurse's job in Colchester and wanted Dave to transfer there but she might as well have been suggesting they emigrate to Outer Mongolia. She should have known that Dave thought he needed a visa and vaccinations if venturing beyond the M25. They were clearly drifting apart at a time when Quinnan was growing closer to Polly Page, who was also the object of Tony Stamp's desire. So when Dave and Polly ended up sleeping

>18 July 2002
The Sun Hill syndicate think they have won the lottery – until Reg Hollis admits he changed one of the numbers that day following a series of coincidences

>23 July 2002
Tony Stamp is accused of sexually abusing a teenage boy

>1 August 2002
Chandler flies into a rage and punches McAllister

As his marriage crumbles, Quinnan begins to wine and dine Polly Page.

together, it not only dealt a hammer blow to his marriage but also to his friendship with Stamp. Polly's fantasy of living happily ever after was quickly revealed to be just that. If love wasn't blind, it was certainly in need of an eye test. Without Jenny, Quinnan began cracking up and had to take two months' sick leave. When on his first day back he witnessed a murder but then proceeded to lose the corpse, some of his colleagues wondered whether he had returned to work too soon. As his private torment continued, he finally decided to accept a job with SO10, the Crime Operations Group. Having reluctantly rejected his last-minute proposal of marriage, Page was heartbroken and, in an uncharacteristic outburst, snapped at

SUN HILL – *The Facts*

Real police officers took such a dim view of previews they were shown from the first series of The Bill that they refused to attend the launch party. The Police Federation later attacked the programme for implying that racial prejudice existed within the force.

the consoling spinster Ackland: 'Do you think I want to end up like you?'

It was a cutting remark, worthy of Vicky Hagen, who jumped ship following the collapse of an affair with Matt Boyden. Although she was a hard-working officer, it had always seemed likely that her colourful private life would curtail her stay at Sun Hill.

>20 August 2002
Reg Hollis is kidnapped and DI Alex Cullen transfers to MIT

>22 August 2002
Luke Ashton and Craig Gilmore exchange a kiss in the sergeant's office

>19 September 2002
Chandler is suspended following Anne Merrick's accusation of rape

Dale Smith can handle himself in most situations.

The Shooting of Bob Cryer

The most surprising departure was that of Bob Cryer, eased out under Chandler's new regime. The unwitting catalyst was PC Dale Smith, himself targeted by Chandler following an incident with black PC Gary McCann. Smith's extreme right-wing views had never endeared him to McCann and when the latter was viciously attacked by a skinhead on the Larkmead Estate, Smith's failure to respond to his call caused questions to be asked. Smith denied the allegations but from that moment Chandler was on his back. Cryer advised him to apply for SO19, the firearms unit, but warned Smith that he would need to launch a charm offensive on Chandler so that the superintendent would support his application.

Smith could easily manage offensive; it was the charm that caused problems.

In fact Chandler saw SO19 as a good way of getting shot of Smith. Now he wanted Cryer out too. In Chandler's eyes, Bob was way past his sell-by date and so he set about making his life hell. Just as Cryer was beginning to wonder whether he was perhaps too old for the job, he was called out to deal with a domestic at a local primary school where he had delivered an anti-drugs talk that morning. An estranged father, Chris Finnessey, had tried to take his son away from the school, only to be thwarted by the boy's teacher, Rachel Bonnington. Cryer attempted to defuse the situation but just as it appeared that everything would be resolved peacefully, Finnessey pulled a knife, held it to Rachel's throat and demanded to see his son. With Finnessey becoming increasingly unbalanced, SO19 were called in. Among their numbers was Dale Smith. When the boy's mother turned up, Finnessey struggled with her in the playground. As Finnessey raised his knife, Smith reckoned he had a clear shot and fired...at the very moment that Cryer chose to throw himself at the attacker. Cryer was hit in the side by

>16 October 2002
Chandler and McAllister marry. In the second episode transmitted that day, Chandler shoots himself

Smith's bullet. Another marksman shot Finnessey dead.

Back at the station, the Relief were puzzled by Cryer's reckless decision to play the hero. Had he been trying to prove to Chandler and co that he wasn't past it? Smith visited him in hospital to apologise, saying that he hadn't even realised he had fired the shot, but Cryer didn't seem to take it in. Facing up to a lengthy spell in a wheelchair, Cryer knew his time was up. Chandler had got his way, although even he would have preferred a less bloody parting.

PC Gary McCann (right) brings in a young suspect.

Reg Hollis's Darkest Hour

If the shooting represented Bob Cryer's darkest hour, Reg Hollis's probably came when he was accused of murder. Reg has been accused of being many things in his time – mostly involving the words 'boring' and 'prat' – but the thought of him as a murderer is about as likely as Jim Carver being hired as a Butlin's Redcoat. Nevertheless when elderly Doreen Tyler, whose flat Reg was about to buy, was

Bob Cryer attempts to defuse the stand-off at school.

Hollis shows surprising pace as he flees the scene of an explosion.

found dead with a head wound, Hollis emerged as the prime suspect, his fingerprints being on the murder weapon, a poker. He was suspended from duty and forced to withdraw his application to transfer as a Royalty Protection Officer with SO14. He began behaving more strangely than usual, while his reluctance to provide an alibi further fuelled suspicion. Eventually a prostitute came forward to say that Hollis had been with her at the time of the murder. He had paid her to talk on the common. His alibi established and the real killer apprehended, Hollis returned to work, although his extra-curricular activities were the talk of the station for weeks to come. As for joining SO14, he decided to withdraw his application. The sigh of relief could be heard all the way from Windsor to Balmoral.

Cass Rickman's Dilemma

Just as some at Sun Hill believed that Hollis had flipped and turned homicidal, there were those who reckoned Cass Rickman had 'gone native'. And in truth it was a close call. Working undercover, she had befriended Leroy Jones, a criminal with connections to Yardies on the Bronte Estate, which was at the centre of a bitter and bloody turf war. To gain Leroy's trust, Cass supplied four black stocking masks and acted as getaway driver when he and his gang robbed a bank but when she found herself falling in love with him, she confessed that she was a police officer. The operation compromised, she came under threat from a Yardie gangster named Toussaint, only for Leroy to shoot him before Toussaint could shoot her. Leroy begged her to go on the run with him. It was a tough choice but, letting her head rule her heart, she decided that her loyalties lay at Sun Hill.

Leroy resurfaced a year later, having been living in South Africa, and tried to pick up the pieces with Rickman. However, he was once again under surveillance by the National Crime Squad on suspicion of heroin smuggling and being involved in the Bronte murders. After a sustained wrestle with her conscience, Rickman was powerless to prevent his arrest but when they met up in his cell they agreed that maybe they'd get together in another life.

The Beech is Back

Don Beech had no qualms about joining the criminal ranks. On the run in Australia, he teamed up with a Vietnamese woman, Frankie Nguyen, to carry out a series of spectacular armed robberies. Claire Stanton doggedly followed him out there to avenge John Boulton's murder but Beech evaded capture by faking his own death when his getaway boat exploded. Returning to London, he master-minded an audacious six-million-pound safe deposit box robbery, which brought him to the attention of Stanton, now working for a security company. As the police closed in, Beech held her captive at gunpoint but just

Leroy Jones points the finger at PC Cass Rickman.

when he looked likely to escape justice once again, she stabbed him in the leg with a hypodermic. Reeling backwards, he dropped the gun. As Stanton picked it up, he urged her to finish him off. However, that was not the kind of justice she wanted. Therefore it was with grim satisfaction that she saw him sent down for life. The game of cat and mouse was finally over. Or was it? With Don Beech you can never be sure.

Taviner Hits Town

Des Taviner. Now he'd have been a match for Beech. Cynical, prejudiced and uncaring, Des's sensitive side went missing around the same time as Shergar. He is only interested in real police work — the rough and tumble on the streets — not being stuck in the CAD room and certainly not dealing with what he considers petty disputes. Des doesn't do domestics. So when Macho Man arrived at Sun Hill to find himself under a gay sergeant (Craig Gilmore) and paired with an old woman (Reg Hollis), he must have thought someone up

SUN HILL – *The Facts*

As a promising young East End boxer, Billy Murray (DS Don Beech) came to know the notorious Kray twins. He used to spar with Charlie Kray who also paid for Murray's first year at drama school.

The haunted face of Nick Klein came to be a familiar sight around Sun Hill.

there was having a laugh at his expense. Once he got to know him, Des came to accept Reg as an occupational hazard but he never made any secret of his distaste for Gilmore, who in turn wasted no opportunity to take Des down a peg or two. As part of his policy of keeping Taviner in check, Gilmore assigned him to look after Special Constable Terry Knowles. Cruising the mean streets with a guy who sold conservatories for a living was not exactly Taviner's idea of fun either.

However, a day trip to the coast was. So when Hollis started brooding about his new girlfriend, Helen, who was attending a weekend conference in Southend, Taviner suggested they take the Area Car to the coast and check her out. While an increasingly irate Gilmore tried to make contact with the missing car, Knowles and PC Nick Klein scoured Sun Hill in search of a conman. Worryingly, Taviner's methods had begun to rub off on the impressionable Knowles – particularly his determination to chat up any pretty girl who crossed his path – so when Knowles spotted an attractive female driver, he persuaded Klein to pull her over on the pretext that she had jumped a red light. Despite Knowles's persistence, the girl proved immune to his charms until he threatened to do a vehicle check. Then she smiled, reached into the glove compartment and produced a steel tail-comb, which she suddenly thrust into the neck of the unsuspecting Knowles before speeding away, leaving him to bleed to death on the pavement.

Taviner and Hollis heard the tragic news when they eventually returned within radio range. Gilmore blamed Taviner for corrupting Knowles and the two came to blows on the day of the funeral before settling on an uneasy truce out of respect to the deceased. It emerged that the killer was a high-class prostitute who had earlier killed her pimp and had a stash of cocaine hidden in the boot of the car. In a coke-induced paranoia, she had wrongly assumed that Knowles knew all about her grisly secrets.

It should have been Chandler. Conway's car explodes.

Conway Killed in Bomb Blast

When it came to paranoia, Knowles's killer had nothing on Chandler. At every turn he saw people plotting against him, mainly because he had so much to hide – including what was by now a full-blown affair with Kate Spears. Intent on monitoring his officers' every move, his control freakery was further fuelled by talk of right-wing extremists marching through Sun Hill. The predominantly Asian Jasmine Allen Estate had already been the target of firebomb attacks, which super-confident DS Vik Singh believed to be racially motivated. When Chandler announced a policy of low-level uniform policing to tackle the problem, Singh reacted angrily and provoked an altercation with a known racist, Simpson, which ended with Singh giving him a sound beating before being dragged away by DC Danny Glaze. The next day a hospitalised Simpson told Singh and Glaze that he didn't intend pressing charges but added ominously that he had other ways of making them pay.

As the racial attacks in the area increased in both number and intensity, Glaze warned Singh that his assault on Simpson was to blame for the escalation of the crisis. This appeared to be borne out when Singh received a parcel containing a bloodied police doll in a cardboard coffin, accompanied by the words 'You Next'. Later that day Singh narrowly

SUN HILL – *The Facts*

Tania Emery, who played ill-fated DC Kate Spears, appeared in the video for Cher's 1996 hit 'One by One'.

Sun Hill erupts in a ball of flame.

escaped when a firebomb was thrown at the Area Car from a passing motorbike. Glaze told him his reckless actions had put every copper in Sun Hill at risk.

Tension remained high following the decision to re-route the march rather than ban it. Chandler was asked to address Asian community leaders but chose to bed Spears and send Conway instead. The meeting passed off satisfactorily but as Conway left the community centre in a panda car, a motorcyclist roared up and the pillion passenger threw a lit petrol bomb through the window of Conway's car. Webb, who had also been at the meeting, could only look on helplessly as the vehicle exploded in a ball of flame.

While the Relief were busy pulling in suspects, Conway's widow, Sandra, waded into Chandler, calling him spineless. The description could also have applied to Singh, who steadfastly refused to accept the consequences of his actions until someone told Webb that the man behind the bombing had recently got a kicking from two black cops in a pub. With the wrath of Meadows about to descend upon his head, Singh finally confessed to the attack on Simpson and tendered his resignation. At least he had the decency to exonerate Glaze.

Taviner lights the blue touch paper.

Taviner's Fatal Miscalculation

Everyone wanted to pay their last respects to Conway. Even Des Taviner, no respecter of authority, was distraught at not having any money to put in the collection. So he confiscated £200 of drug money from a young suspect and put part of it into Conway's pot, little realising that the notes were forgeries.

SUN HILL – *The Facts*

When filming on location, The Bill does not have permission to use sirens. These are added in the dubbing suite.

When he learned the truth, he knew he must remove the notes or he would have a lot of explaining to do.

After weeks of speculation as to the identity of Chandler's secret lover, Webb caught him playing tonsil hockey with Spears. Accusing Chandler of fiddling while Conway burned, Webb wondered aloud what the Yard would think of their Sun Hill sleaze buster basking in his

PC Ben Hayward was among the victims of the blast.

Ackland was lured into a trap and tied with her own cuffs by three thugs. Carver raced to the rescue and went berserk, taking on all comers, following which Chandler finally gave the order to send in the Territorial Support Group.

With the situation seemingly under control, Chandler stood down his team. Uniform shared a bottle of scotch with CID in their office and raised a toast to 'ordinary, decent coppers'. But while Ackland and Carver exchanged a furtive kiss in the dark and half a dozen more officers stayed behind for another drink, Taviner was preoccupied with getting at the counterfeit £50 notes in Conway's fund, which was sitting in Monroe's office. After trying unsuccessfully to force Monroe's window from the outside, he spotted a masked man throwing a petrol bomb at the station. Then as a thug climbed over the wall, Taviner grabbed his bag, lit the petrol bomb inside it and, seen only by PC Sam Harker from the station balcony, lobbed it through Monroe's window with the intention of reducing the incriminating notes to ashes. What he didn't know was that Harry Fullerton, who had been decorating the station, had stored his welding equipment in there. The bomb ignited Fullerton's gas bottle and within seconds the entire station was engulfed in an almighty fireball.

As scene examiners picked through the

own mire. Now that their secret was out, Chandler didn't want to know. Realising she had been little more than Chandler's plaything, Spears vowed to reveal to everyone at Sun Hill what their leader was really like. She told him his career would be finished.

News that the march had been banned after all stirred up a furious backlash from neo-Nazi thugs. In response gangs of Asian youths also took to the streets. Trouble was kicking off all over Sun Hill as Chandler adhered to his policy of low-profile policing. Those on patrol ran a gauntlet of hate. Chasing a youth who had fired ball bearings at her from a slingshot,

station ashes, Chandler informed the Relief that Inspector Monroe, DC Paul Riley, PC Di Worrell and PC Ben Hayward were all dead on arrival at St. Hugh's. Spears and Harker were both in a critical condition while Taviner and Page (who, still grieving over Quinnan, had taken an overdose) were detained under observation. Cass Rickman, who had cruelly rebuffed Harker minutes before the blast, waited anxiously at his bedside, as did Taviner...but for different reasons. For Harker was the only witness. Back at the remains of the station, Webb fretted for news of Spears. Shortly before the blast, she had told him she was finished with Chandler and had invited him to take the super's place. Webb had been overjoyed; now he just felt empty inside. When word came through that Spears had died before being able to dish the dirt on Chandler, Webb went AWOL, returning to heckle Chandler's press conference, where he merely succeeded in making a fool of himself. His other mistake was to tell McAllister about Chandler's affair, a revelation that made her eyes light up. Ever willing to turn a tragedy to her own advantage, the scheming McAllister confided to Chandler that she knew all about him and Spears, but not to worry because his secret was safe with her.

Taviner's torment showed no signs of abating, reaching the stage where he considered switching off Harker's life-support system but

was unable to go through with it. He was just about to unburden himself to Hollis when a tearful Rickman reported that Harker had suffered a fatal cardiac arrest. Taviner's relief lasted only as long as it took Chandler to tell him to carry the memorial flag at the service and for MIT to voice their suspicions that the bombing may have been an inside job. At the end of the service, McAllister sidled up to Chandler, purportedly to congratulate him on his speech but in reality to offer him sex on a plate. When he expressed interest, she dragged him into the disabled toilet. Meanwhile Taviner feared the worst on hearing that MIT wanted to re-interview him but was spared by the

DCI Marsden (James Macpherson) is quizzed by Meadows about Chandler's past.

shock news that Fullerton had confessed to burning down the station.

Although Fullerton also confessed to Conway's murder, Glaze was certain that Simpson was behind the attacks. In a rare display of conscience Taviner, too, seemed keen to get Fullerton off the hook and between them they proved that he was a fantasist not a killer. Determined that Simpson should go down for the murders, Taviner planted incriminating evidence, as a result of which Simpson was charged. He claimed that he had been fitted up.

Investigating Chandler

McAllister wasted little time in turning her special relationship with Chandler to her own ends and when a younger model joined CID in the form of DC Eva Sharpe, a jealous McAllister asked Chandler to transfer the newcomer to June Ackland's pioneering Community Safety Unit. When Chandler stalled, McAllister pushed the matter too far and, acting on Cullen's advice, he dumped her. If he thought that was the end of the matter, he was sorely mistaken. After a week off sick, McAllister returned to work to tell Chandler that she was pregnant – and that he was the father.

Cullen also tipped Chandler off that Meadows and Webb were plotting something. Ever since discovering Chandler's sordid secret with Spears, Webb had been intent on bringing him down and, perhaps to his surprise, had found a willing ally in Meadows. Webb began digging into Chandler's past, tracking down colleagues from his days at Hendon, including Taviner, who recalled something strange happening with Chandler's girlfriend at the time and put Webb on to DCI Peter Marsden – Chandler's best friend at Hendon. Without going into details, Marsden confirmed that a traumatic event had occurred, adding that he and Chandler hadn't spoken since. Webb was more intrigued than ever. Back at Sun Hill, Chandler felt obliged to call a halt to speculation surrounding his whereabouts on the night of Conway's murder by naming Cullen as his alibi. Meadows didn't buy it and Cullen was none too happy to be drawn into the conspiracy. The hounds would not be thrown off the scent that easily.

Nick Klein's Secret

Slowly things at the station began to return to normal. Klein had often taken recreational drugs and, to forget the misery of the past few weeks, he and Rickman went clubbing. Klein's supplier ensured that both officers got as high as a kite. Party-girl Rickman was all for another night on the town but it turned sour when Rob Ingram, a guy she had met in an Irish pub, collapsed and died after taking drugs. As her thoughts turned back to Harker, she told Klein she was never touching drugs again. However, to her horror she realised she had left her bag in the club. Inside was her warrant card…alongside an ecstasy tablet. Luckily the

SUN HILL – The Facts

The first acting job for Rene Zagger (PC Nick Klein) was in a pop video for Wet Wet Wet playing a young Marti Pellow.

Klein and Rickman go clubbing.

purse was handed in at the front desk to one of the new arrivals, PC Cathy Bradford, who told Rickman that she had flushed the tab down the loo – but reminded Rickman that now she owed her. Similarly Klein found himself in the pocket of the flashy new DS, Phil Hunter, after a dealer had revealed selling drugs to an officer at Sun Hill. Hunter persuaded the dealer to drop the allegation but let Klein know that he expected favours in return.

Matt Boyden and Craig Gilmore were never likely to be bosom buddies but Boyden's scarcely concealed hostility towards the gay sergeant shocked the rest of the Relief. Gilmore decided to get his own back by

Connie Hyde, who plays Cathy Bradford, in
an earlier **The Bill** *role.*

coming on strong to Boyden. Hugely embarrassed by Gilmore propositioning him, Boyden agreed to a truce. They soon had a weightier problem to deal with – namely a tough new inspector, Gina Gold, who could

Gina Gold knows the way to a man's heart.

Ashton, and DC Ken Drummond – shirts by Thomas Magnum, waistline by Frank Cannon.

Then there was Kerry Young. Klein and Rickman were out clubbing one night when Klein spotted a pretty blonde who told him she was a hairdresser. Using his best chat-up line, he said he was a pilot and allowed her to play with his joystick in an adjoining alley. The following morning he discovered that last night's shag was Sun Hill's new PC, who in turn was equally surprised to find that her hero of the skies was permanently grounded in Canley High Street...

Stamp Fights to Clear his Name

Through organising a community football match, Tony Stamp befriended troubled teenager Lee Dwyer, who repaid the trust by nominating Stamp for Community Bobby of the Year. When Lee was threatened with exclusion from school for trashing the toilets, Stamp successfully argued that he was a good kid who deserved a second chance. Claiming that his stepfather, Darren Saunders, had thrown him out, Lee turned up on Stamp's doorstep, begging to use the toilet. Stamp reluctantly allowed him in but drove the boy straight home afterwards. A couple of days later the stepfather barged into the station and accused Stamp of sexually abusing Lee. Suspended from duty, Stamp pleaded his innocence but Lee insisted that he had been lured into Stamp's house to watch videos. A medical examination confirmed that he had been sexually abused. Stamp's anguish deepened when Jim Carver, in his role as the CSU's Family Liaison Officer, appeared to be

have eaten both of them for breakfast. This was one woman with whom even Boyden wasn't going to chance his luck. She quickly left her mark on Ackland, implying that she thought both June and the CSU were a waste of time. Having got off on the wrong foot, Ackland tried to start again but Gold crushingly informed her that she had no intention of being 'nice'. Among other new recruits were rookie PC Gary Best, trainee DC Brandon Kane, the returning Luke

PC Kerry Young finds herself in a tricky predicament.

siding with Saunders. Even after Lee suddenly withdrew the allegation, Stamp was devastated to hear from Carver that he wasn't in the clear yet, that he was in effect guilty until proven innocent. As he returned home, a sad and forlorn figure, Stamp's world plummeted to an all-time low when a brick was hurled through

SUN HILL – *The Facts*

Melanie, the crooked nightclub hostess who enjoyed a lesbian romp with PC Gemma Osbourne in 2002, was played by Jaime Murray, daughter of Billy Murray (Don Beech).

his window. He instinctively went to phone the police but hung up on seeing an attached note bearing the word 'Pervert'. Stamp's luck only began to change when Kane replaced Carver as FLO and revealed the abuser to be Lee's real father, Steve Dwyer. Stamp returned to work, relieved at being cleared but incensed at having been mistrusted by people whom he had previously counted as friends. Carver coldly replied that he had only been doing his job.

The Fall of Chandler

Chandler was starting to feel the heat. He had heard that Meadows and Webb had been making inquiries about the disappearance of his

Tony Stamp battles to prove his innocence.

Cullen owed him for covering up a death in custody years ago; Cullen maintained he had paid his debt by concealing the fact that Chandler had raped someone. Bristling with anger, Chandler then heard that Cullen wanted to transfer to MIT. Aware that he dared not block the move for fear of being deafened by the din of skeletons falling out of his closet, Chandler had no option but to push it through with indecent haste.

Chandler's discomfort was matched by that of Taviner. Convinced that Taviner had set him up for

ex-girlfriend from Hendon but bluffed his way out of it by maintaining that the secret in question concerned the suicide of Marsden's sister Louise. Also there was the small matter of McAllister's baby. Chandler ordered her to have an abortion but she backed out at the last minute. When she showed Chandler the ultrasound picture of the baby, he flew into a rage and tried to flush the picture down the toilet. As McAllister attempted to retrieve it, he lashed out at her and sent her crashing to the floor, leaving her to explain away a black eye in CID the next day. Knowing Chandler of old, Cullen immediately accused him of being responsible for McAllister's bruising and warned that he wasn't prepared to help him in future. In the ensuing argument, Chandler said

the petrol bombing of Sun Hill, Simpson sent his hired thugs to coerce him into telling the truth at the forthcoming murder trial. Taviner resisted until, on the eve of the trial, Simpson's men kidnapped Hollis and took him to a disused slaughterhouse. CID knew they were dealing with unstable individuals. After all, no one in their right mind would choose to spend time alone with Hollis! Praying that his buddy would somehow survive, Taviner went ahead with his false testimony, prompting Simpson to change his plea to guilty. And the resourceful Hollis managed to escape by convincing one kidnapper of the error of his ways and by setting fire to the slaughterhouse before his accomplice could deliver the killer blow. Hollis later recounted

Kidnapped by hired thugs, Hollis managed to talk his way out of trouble in his own inimitable way.

the story of his psychological triumph in full detail to anybody who would listen. Only the slide show was missing.

Luke Ashton was a confused young man. Despite going out on a few dates with Kerry Young, he found himself strangely drawn to Sgt. Gilmore. The feeling was mutual and the pair ended up enjoying a passionate kiss at the station. Gilmore wanted more but Ashton was in denial, insisting that he was a red-blooded heterosexual. Poor Gilmore could only watch and suffer as Ashton paraded the physicality of his relationship with Young under the sergeant's nose.

Webb's research into Chandler's ex-girlfriend from Hendon had thrown up a name, Anne Merrick. Evasive at first, she opened up to reveal that Louise Marsden had committed suicide 20 years ago after claiming to have been raped at a party. Among the men Louise

SUN HILL – *The Facts*

Natalie Roles (DS Debbie McAllister) is a keen mountaineer who recently reached the 19,000 ft summit of Africa's Mount Kilimanjaro. Suzanne Maddock (PC Cass Rickman) also reached the summit.

Chandler would not take 'no' for an answer from his pregnant bride on their wedding night.

had accused of raping her was Chandler. Disobeying Meadows' orders, Webb confronted Peter Marsden with the allegation. He in turn went to see Chandler, who dismissed it out of hand, saying that Anne Merrick was mentally ill. In a state of barely controlled panic, Chandler then called on Anne, hoping to convince her that her memory was unreliable. Later that day she went to Sun Hill to report that Chandler had just raped her.

Suspended from duty, Chandler denied everything and begged McAllister to give him an alibi. To prove how serious he was about their relationship, he asked her to marry him. She agreed, but pointed out bluntly that it was merely an arrangement between two desperate people. Quizzed by CIB, McAllister not only supported Chandler's alibi but also confessed that she was pregnant with his child, and when forensic evidence showed that Anne had not been sexually assaulted, the charge against Chandler was dropped. The next day Anne Merrick was found dead.

Chandler set about covering his tracks over the Louise Marsden affair by asking his old pals – among them the now Deputy Assistant Commissioner Gordon Cooper – to keep quiet. He then visited his drunken brother James – the only other witness to the Marsden rape – and tried to buy his silence. James appeared reluctant, so Chandler beat him up. When Meadows and Webb caught up with him, James confessed to having seen Chandler rape Louise Marsden and eventually agreed to make a statement to that effect. Chandler had one last trick up his sleeve. Knowing that Meadows was fond of McAllister, he announced that they were about to get married. Meadows was uneasy about taking McAllister down with Chandler so he locked James's statement in his desk. However, Webb was not prepared to let it lie and, retrieving the statement, notified Internal Investigations.

Backed into a corner, Chandler prepares to die.

Chandler and McAllister were duly married. He marked their wedding night by brutally forcing her to have sex with him even though he had previously agreed to wait until after the baby was born. The following morning DCC Cooper informed Chandler that he'd had a visit from CIB and that the game was up. Meanwhile McAllister stumbled across a photocopy of James Chandler's statement and that, allied to her treatment the night before, led her to conclude that Chandler really was a rapist. As they argued bitterly in the office, Chandler suddenly pulled a gun – brought in from a shooting on the Bronte – and threatened to kill her, the baby and then himself. The stress sent McAllister into premature labour. Learning that Chandler had a gun, Meadows barged in to the office and tried to persuade him to hand himself over quietly. Instead the disgraced superintendent blew his own brains out.

MARK WINGETT

As an expert scuba diver, Mark Wingett is used to making surprising discoveries but he is unlikely to forget the time he got that sinking feeling while filming a scene for *The Bill* in a sewer. 'It was in the early half-hour episodes,' remembers Mark, 'and we were filming at a huge Victorian house in Ladbroke Grove.

'The idea was that the house was being raided for drugs, which got flushed down the toilet, but Carver, anticipating this, was waiting at the drain at the back of the house to recover the evidence. Unfortunately, as a filming unit we didn't have control of the whole house and, unbeknown to us, someone in the house had just been to the loo. So as I reached down for

Mark was born in landlocked Leicestershire but his father was a naval officer and the family ended up living in such diverse locations as Malta, Singapore and Portsmouth. Mark always nurtured acting ambitions even though a school questionnaire led the careers officer to conclude that the job he was best suited for was that of zookeeper. Undeterred,

INTERVIEW

the supposed drugs I ended up with a handful of sh*t instead. It was absolutely disgusting. So much for the glamorous life of an actor.'

Mark joined the National Youth Theatre and went on to play a mod in The Who's rock opera *Quadrophenia*. While appearing as a paratrooper in a Tony Marchant play at the Royal Court Theatre, he was plucked for *The Bill* forerunner *Woodentop* along with Gary Olsen (PC Dave Litten) and Robert Pugh (the original DI Roy Galloway). 'Until then I'd always played characters on the other side of the law. For example I was a kidnapper in *Fox*, where Trudie

Jim and Tosh spring into action.

as PC Jim Carver

Goodwin was also in the cast. Anyway I did the pilot, forgot all about it and went off to do other things. Little did I know that Jim Carver would become a big part of my life.

'My brother Matthew has written some episodes of *The Bill* and it was he who drew my attention to the fact that Carver can react in any number of ways in a given situation. Jim's not a bad bloke but he is committed and takes the job very seriously. I'm not sure whether or not I actually like him. And life's a problem for him because if you're an alcoholic you never get over it. That was the downfall of his relationship

with June. He proposed to her while he was drunk but when he sobered up he changed his mind.

'The alcoholism storyline has been great fun – to be able to do the behaviour without suffering the hangover. And since doing the research I don't drink any more! It came about when Richard Handford, who was the executive producer, had the idea of putting Carver back into uniform. My first reaction was that I didn't want to go back into uniform – it was like demotion and I took it personally. Then I thought about it and reckoned we could give Carver a real problem with this. Why not make him an alcoholic? This was shortly after Kevin Lloyd, who had a serious drink problem, had passed away. The company really supported Kevin, who was a fantastic actor and a lovely man, so I decided to do it as a tribute to him. The storyline got a fantastic response from the public and people would yell at me in the street: "Have you had a drink yet, mate?"

'I also get a good reaction from the police about Carver. They know me by name, which is nice but surprising because they only usually know you by name if you're on file. The only criticism they ever make is that we don't show all the paperwork, but I explain that *The Bill* is a drama and that poring over paperwork is not exactly dramatic. I think we get things pretty much right and to my mind one of the successes of the show is the large rotation of characters and the way it has adapted to different changes of format. Having said that, with everything that goes on in the place, I really wouldn't want to live in Sun Hill!'

THE NEW BROOM

Adam Okaro, the new superintendent at Sun Hill, had a reputation for being calm in a crisis. But with his officers' complex private lives threatening to destroy the working fabric of the station, Claire Rayner might have been a wiser appointment. Ackland and Carver had moved in together but were bringing their domestic problems to the office; Ashton had decided that the best way to shake off Gilmore was to announce that he was getting engaged to Young; Klein had been caught on CCTV taking drugs by Hunter who was now blackmailing him; Taviner had tried to kill himself after finally admitting to Hollis that he threw the petrol bomb; McAllister had just given birth to a baby boy by a dead father; oh, and there was a serial killer on the loose. Welcome to Sun Hill!

The Sun Hill Serial Killer

The body of Vicky Casson was the sixth to be washed up on the banks of the Thames in the space of four months. There were three prime suspects – Shane Pellow, a seedy undertaker and S&M enthusiast who had links with a number of the previous victims and was the boyfriend of the first, Liz Chambers; Martin Porter, a violent solicitor and former boyfriend of Kerry Young; and Simon Kitson, a persistent local journalist who had been dating Cass Rickman and seemed to know a lot of private information about the victims. Also there was the mysterious disappearance of his first wife.

To take everyone's

Luke and Kerry: a doomed union.

>23 October 2002
PC Gemma Osbourne books into Sun Hill

>7 November 2002
Arrival of Adam Okaro, the new superintendent

>12 December 2002
PC Cass Rickman becomes the final victim of the Sun Hill serial killer

Robbie Cryer, niece of Bob, presides over Cop Idol.

minds off such an awful year, the new civilian front desk officer Robbie Cryer (niece of Bob) organised a pre-Christmas talent contest, Cop Idol. The hugely anticipated star turn was to be Robbie, Cass Rickman and Kerry Young in a tribute to Atomic Kitten…but Rickman was abducted on her way to finish her relationship with Simon Kitson once and for all. When she was driven to a deserted warehouse, blindfolded and had chunks of her hair hacked off, it dawned on her that she was in the hands of the Sun Hill serial killer.

Oblivious to Rickman's fate, Young and Ashton handed out wedding invitations while Klein, ever more addicted to cocaine and desperate to free himself from Hunter's hold, discovered that among the DS's many female

SUN HILL – *The Facts*

Cyril Nri (Superintendent Adam Okaro) has appeared twice before in The Bill, firstly as a barrister and secondly as a Rwandan refugee. But he is no stranger to police roles, having played DC Burton who investigated the shooting of Phil Mitchell in EastEnders.

conquests was the wife of a dangerous boxing promoter. Klein reasoned that the husband would be less than happy to learn what had been going on behind his back and in his bed. Faced with compelling evidence, Hunter agreed to call it quits. Klein may have been rid of one gremlin but Cass's disappearance hardly put him in the mood to celebrate. When

>2 January 2003
  The wedding of PCs Kerry Young and Luke Ashton

>30 January 2003
  Aussie PC Cameron Tait signs on at Sun Hill

>12 February 2003
  Sgt. Sheelagh Murphy replaces Craig Gilmore

Cass Rickman's relationship with journalist Simon Kitson turned out to be the death of her.

SUN HILL – *The Facts*

Georgia Moffett, who plays teenage temptress Abigail Nixon, comes from a family of actors, her parents being Peter Davison and Sandra Dickinson. She originally auditioned for The Bill as one of the victims of the Sun Hill serial killer.

Rickman's bag was brought in and there was no sign of her at her flat, Klein responded to reports of a floating body by searching the waterfront. After a few minutes he spotted something in the water. It was Rickman's naked corpse. The serial killer had struck again.

Simon Kitson quickly emerged as the chief suspect. A strand of Rickman's hair was found in the boot of the car Simon was driving and his sister Pat said that he hadn't returned home the previous night. Simon was detained overnight for questioning and a grief-stricken Klein was appalled at having to serve him dinner in his cell. As he lay down the tray, Klein deliberately broke the plastic knife and told Simon that he would be better off dead. Shortly afterwards Simon was found with his wrists slashed.

To most of the officers at Sun Hill, Simon Kitson's suicide was tantamount to a confession. An exception was Alex Cullen's

>**27 February 2003**
DC Eva Sharpe's missing daughter Joanna is found alive

>**19 March 2003**
Sgt Matt Boyden has sex with 15-year-old Abigail Nixon, daughter of DI Samantha Nixon

>**1 May 2003**
Sgt Matt Boyden is murdered

successor, Acting DI Samantha Nixon, who went against the flow with her gut instinct that the serial killer was still out there. Pat Kitson was adamant that her brother was innocent and became involved in an undignified brawl with Klein at Rickman's Liverpool funeral, which sent the coffin toppling to the ground. Afterwards they comforted each other in a moment of shared grief. Nixon stuck to her guns and was rewarded when a prostitute came forward to provide Simon with an alibi for the night of Rickman's murder. Discussing the case with Lennox (for whom this was a last investigation before joining MIT), Nixon suggested that the killer was obsessed with Simon and might try to harm another police officer because he had died in custody. Perhaps, she added, Simon had killed himself to protect someone close to him.

Going solo, Nixon responded to a text message from Pat Kitson and went to a Thames-side warehouse. Finding Rickman's chain and a ligature (all of the victims had been strangled) but no sign of Pat, Nixon phoned Lennox to report that she had unearthed the murder site but as she did so Pat crept up from behind and felled her with a blow to the head. With Nixon tied to a chair in an attic, Lennox discovered her mobile phone at the warehouse and recognised the last number dialled – Pat Kitson's. The captive Nixon asked Pat why she had killed so many women. Pat revealed that she and her brother had been lovers but they were caught and she was sent away. Her first victim was Simon's wife and after that she killed everyone who became involved with him so that he would be more

dependent on her. Just as she tightened the ligature ready to add Nixon to the list, Lennox burst in and overpowered her. For once in his life his timing was immaculate.

A grief-stricken Nick Klein at Rickman's funeral.

Crazy Cathy Bradford

Not all of the psychopaths around Sun Hill were on the wrong side of the law. Take PC Cathy Bradford. Her behaviour had always been irrational but she became a candidate for the men in white coats when, having been given the all-clear after being stabbed with a heroin needle by a vagrant, she announced to the world that she was HIV positive. Fortunately, Robbie Cryer saw through the sham and forced Bradford to backtrack and pretend there had been a mix-up over her results. One of the few people who had any

Acting DI Samantha Nixon trapped the serial killer.

that she was pregnant with his child. In another desperate attempt to win his sympathy, she invented a story about being attacked by a mystery stalker...until it transpired that her injuries were self-inflicted.

Kerry Dumps Luke

The course of true love was even bumpier for Luke Ashton and Kerry Young. Ashton's long-lost father threatened to spoil the big day, unaware that his son was perfectly capable of doing it for himself. For after an eventful stag night (during which Matt Boyden was tied naked to a lamp-post and his photo posted on the station notice board above the caption 'Does my bum look big in this?') Ashton ended up in bed with Gilmore. Gina Gold discovered them in the morning and tore Gilmore off a strip. He offered to apply for a transfer but Gold refused to accept it, insisting, however, that he steered clear of Ashton in future. As it was, Ashton turned up for the wedding with a black eye after arresting a mugger on the way to the church. On his return from honeymoon, Ashton was forced to face up to reality after being attracted to Joe Kincaid, a young solicitor in an assault case. He resolved to reveal his secret to his bride of two weeks but before he could do so, she said she had news of her own – she was pregnant.

Gilmore could not bear to see Luke living a lie and unwittingly dropped a hint to Kerry about her husband's sexuality. After receiving a severe beating while guarding a suspect in hospital, Gilmore faced months off work and decided to press ahead with his transfer. This time Gold did not stand in his way – on

time for her was Brandon Kane but he made the fatal mistake of cooling on her after their one-night stand. Or rather it was fatal for Kane's wife, who was pushed down the stairs by the obsessive Bradford. With Kane under suspicion, Crazy Cathy tried to get him off the hook by saying that he had been with her at the time of the murder before then claiming

Fatal attraction: Brandon Kane cannot see through crazy Cathy Bradford.

condition that he told Kerry her fears were groundless, that Luke was straight. Perhaps because it was what she wanted to hear, Kerry accepted the explanation but a chance meeting with Joe Kincaid wrecked her game of Happy Families. Confronted with Joe's version of events, Luke broke down and admitted to Kerry that he was gay. A distraught Kerry decided to have a termination but Luke begged her to keep the baby. She relented, only to miscarry shortly afterwards. Now, she said, there was nothing to keep them together.

Hunter Becomes the Hunted

Phil Hunter was in deep with local drugs baron Ron Gregory. As punishment for not tipping Gregory off about a police raid, Hunter was forced to allow his wife Cindy to spend the night with the villain. They didn't have sex but Gregory took degrading photos of her...to be used if and when required. Okaro and Meadows had worked out that Hunter was on Gregory's payroll and decided to give him enough rope to hang himself. Okaro wanted to target the major dealers – people like Gregory – and controversially ordered his officers to ignore anyone who was simply in possession of drugs. The vindictive Bradford anonymously phoned the Commissioner's office to report Okaro's edict and when his liberal views on drugs were reported in the press, he found his job in jeopardy. Borough Commander Jane Fitzwilliam angrily instructed him to toe the line, whereupon he handed her his resignation.

Together they went to Scotland Yard where, to Okaro's surprise, the ice maiden defended him to the Commander, saying that he had shown full commitment to serving his community. As they left, she told him she had torn up his resignation.

Not surprisingly given the part he played in the downfall of his predecessor, Okaro was a little wary of Meadows at first but was soon impressed by the way he operated. For his part, Meadows only had eyes for femme fatale Debbie McAllister. Ever since persuading her not to have baby Andrew adopted, Meadows had grown closer to McAllister. Convinced that McAllister was the latest in the long line of her husband's mistresses, Laura Meadows confronted him at work but he brushed her aside and shortly afterwards announced that he had left her. He then made his move on McAllister but she was playing it uncharacteristically cool.

The Paedophile Ring

Meadows was alarmed to hear that an old family friend, Judge Howard Sinclair, was suspected of corruption. Worse was to follow when Sinclair and local businessman Clive Inverdale became implicated in a paedophile ring. Before he could face the music, Sinclair gassed himself and Inverdale was gunned

With Gilmore in attendance, a black eye was the least of Luke Ashton's problems on his wedding day.

Greedy DS Phil Hunter (right) proved easy prey for Ron Gregory (Jesse Birdsall).

down by a hitman while making his first appearance in court. All the clues suggested that Hunter's chum, Ron Gregory, was behind the contract killing. Even Hunter was sickened to think that Gregory could be a paedophile, the case taking on a new significance for the officers at Sun Hill when DC Eva Sharpe's young daughter Joanna went missing during an Open Day at the station. Happily, she was eventually found safe and well; another little black girl was less fortunate.

Bringing Gregory to justice became the number one priority but he was a cool customer and had the perfect alibi for the time of the hit on Inverdale – he was with the gullible Hunter, who had allowed himself to be used. Gregory tried to secure Hunter's loyalty by reminding him of the photographs

of Cindy but, under increasing pressure from above, Hunter showed them to Meadows. Now Meadows understood how Gregory was able to exercise such a hold over the DS. Gregory had one more test for Hunter. Appearing with a nine-year-old girl, he ordered Hunter to have sex with her. Hunter immediately called Nixon but Gregory, backed by his ever-present solicitor, pointed out that the girl was his niece and that Hunter must have got the wrong end of the stick. It had been a trap, and now Gregory

SUN HILL – *The Facts*

While living in Hollywood for three months, Chris Simmons, who plays DC Mickey Webb, was the only British actor to feature in the docu-soap Desperately Seeking Stardom.

Webb watches in disbelief as Okaro hands over his own daughter to a suspected paedophile.

knew for certain that he could no longer trust his tame detective. So he phoned the contract killer to place an order for two more jobs – this time the targets were to be Hunter and Cindy.

Following up a lead on the case, Webb watched in horror as Okaro handed over his daughter to a suspect at a children's playground. Was Okaro involved in the paedophile ring? Before Webb could get his head around the idea, it emerged that the

SUN HILL – *The Facts*

Tony Blair and his family recently came out as fans of **The Bill.**

'suspect' was an undercover cop and that by going it alone, Webb had screwed up a fresh operation to nail Gregory. Determined to make amends, Webb enlisted the help of Robbie Cryer to break into the home of Gregory's solicitor, where they found a child locked in the attic. Gregory's unexpected return left them staring down the barrel of a gun but luckily Hunter came good when he was really needed and the Sun Hill cavalry arrived in the nick of time. The ring was smashed.

Secrets and Lies

After the break-up of his marriage, Meadows had started seeing a prostitute. Webb was

New sergeant Sheelagh Murphy fell pregnant by Des Taviner.

investigating a series of date rapes but without much luck or sympathy – he reckoned the girls were asking for it – until one of the victims was Laura Meadows, attacked by a man she had invited into her home after meeting him on the Internet. Webb's myopic view of rape victims was dealt a more permanent blow when he went in pursuit of a gang of thugs. He was overpowered, handcuffed with his own cuffs and then brutally raped. His life in turmoil, he finally broke down and told Meadows but chose to walk out of Sun Hill rather than face the Force Medical Examiner.

Although Des Taviner's appeal to women remained a closely guarded secret, he wasted no time in bedding the new station sergeant, Sheelagh Murphy. However the tryst backfired when Murphy discovered she was pregnant…and Des was the father. Yet that was the least of Taviner's problems. For when the racist thug Simpson, whom Taviner had framed for the bombing of Sun Hill, hired a private investigator to find evidence to support a possible appeal, the truth about Des's involvement emerged at last. As the net closed in, Danny Glaze fled to South Africa and Taviner confessed his sins to Murphy. In the mistaken belief that Murphy had told Okaro, the tormented Taviner drove into a burning building with Hollis in the passenger seat. Reg pulled through but was in hospital for weeks; Des's body was never found.

Taviner's death was the second to hit Sun Hill in the space of a few months, Matt Boyden having been shot after making one enemy too many. The queue of people waiting to take a pop at him stretched right down Canley High Street.

Heartbreak for June

Life was scarcely any kinder to June Ackland. Carver's alcoholism was proving an insurmountable barrier in their relationship.

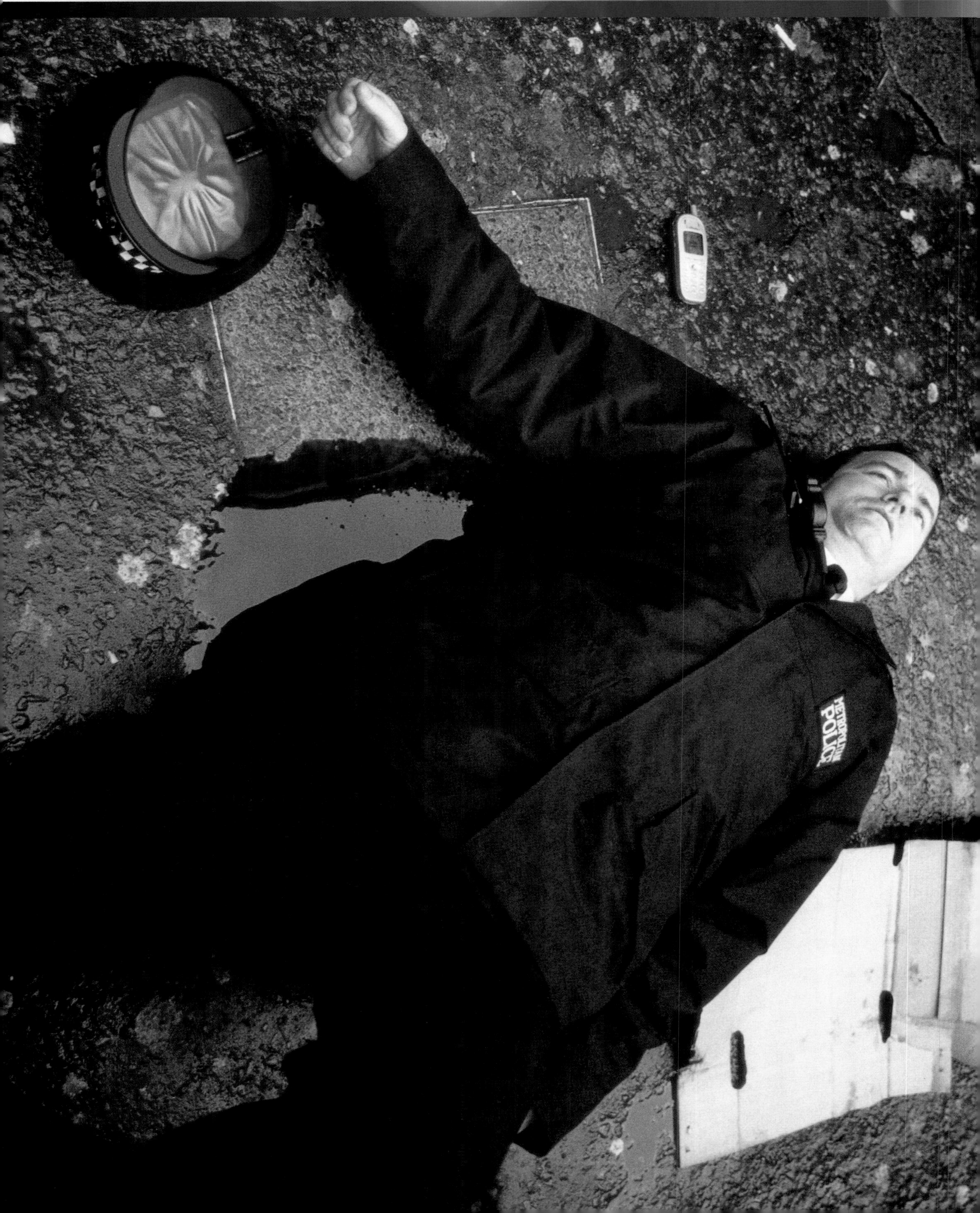
METROPOLITAN
POLICE

Jim Carver manages a rare smile for his wedding day. The same can't be said for the bride.

Clutching at enough straws to make a basket, June still nurtured hopes of dragging him up the aisle before opening time, all the more so when she discovered an engagement ring in his desk. However it was not for her at all – but for Marie Graham, one of his Family Liaison clients. Even for someone to whom misfortune was such a frequent visitor, June found Carver's wedding hard to stomach. Deciding she had suffered enough, she left early, only to be dragged into bushes and attacked. A passer-by appeared on the scene before mysteriously vanishing. Weeks later the same man turned up at Sun Hill – he was probationary PC Gabriel Kent. He asked whether a June Ackland worked there but when Ackland recognised him, he claimed never to have seen her before. The sinister Kent took to psychologically bullying Gina Gold and turned Okaro and the entire Relief against her. When Gold was breathalysed after a traffic accident, the Relief covered it up but Kent discovered the truth and used the information to strengthen his hold over her. He clearly has a hidden agenda. With Bradford and Kent at large in the same station and a hearse parked in the yard on permanent standby, Sun Hill remains the posting from hell.

Matt Boyden lies dead in the street, gunned down on the orders of his daughter Amy.

SUN HILL – *The Facts*

By the end of 2003, there will have been over 1,800 episodes of The Bill.

Carver's marriage was doomed from the outset. The unstable Marie had a previous conviction for criminal damage and was also a heavy drinker. Indeed it soon became apparent that alcoholism (recovering in Carver's case) was about the only thing they had in common. She convinced herself that Jim was still seeing June and took to turning up unexpectedly at the station to check on him. Although her visits were not always voluntary — after trashing a cinema toilet, she was brought in on a drunk and disorderly charge and had to be forcibly restrained by her embarassed husband.

Undeterred, Marie began stalking June and issuing threats. The more paranoid Marie became, the more violent she was and the loyal Carver served as the hapless punchbag. One particularly aggressive 'domestic' ended when Gabriel Kent intervened, attacking them both and smashing Carver over the head with a vodka bottle. Although not denying the fight, Marie insisted that she had not caused Carver's head and facial injuries, but nobody believed that Gabriel had been responsible for the assault. Carver was appalled by the prospect of bringing charges against his own wife but realised that drastic action was needed to save Marie from herself. Reluctantly he pressed ahead with the case and Marie was charged with actual bodily harm. After initially vowing to fight dirty, she pleaded guilty and even hoped for reconciliation, but Carver decided that he had suffered enough. It just wouldn't work.

Mother Love

Sly and manipulative, Kent was proving an accomplished liar, his unchanging facial expression rarely giving a clue to any inner feelings. He was very much a mystery wrapped inside an enigma. Several members of the relief soon had cause to distrust him but nothing ever stuck. He developed a keen interest in June Ackland who, after her experience with Carver, was naturally wary about embarking on another relationship with a work colleague. But Kent was nothing if not persistent and with June at her most vulnerable, charmed her into bed.

Gina Gold and the returning Dale Smith (now a sergeant) had both crossed swords with Kent and

Carver and June's romantic past fed Marie's paranoia.

Gabriel Kent set his sights on June.

were on a mission to uncover the truth about him. Delving into his background, they discovered that Gabriel Kent was June's son whom she had given away for adoption when she was 16 and had not seen since. When the news reached Carver's ears, he felt obliged to tell her. Not surprisingly, June was horrified and told Gabriel that she wanted nothing more to do with him, but he eventually confessed that he wasn't her son at all. In truth, Gabriel's adoptive brother was June's real son. Gabriel gave her the address and, acting on the pretext of being interested in buying the house, June came face to face with her long-lost son. Part of her desperately wanted to reveal her true identity, but she thought better of it and left without blowing her cover.

Gabriel's unmasking merely heightened the bad blood between him and Carver and when Jim was struggling for his life following an incident at a local swimming pool, Gabriel thought twice before diving in to rescue him from drowning. Thereafter the pair reached an uneasy truce.

Polly's Predicament
Ever since the fatal Sun Hill fire, Polly Page had struggled to get her life together. After being put on long-term leave, she returned to the station as part of the Community Safety Unit. Her compassion for humanity manifested itself when she befriended Dr Owen Preston, whose wife had been murdered and who himself had been diagnosed with an incurable

brain tumour. If Page was somewhat naïve in accepting Dr Preston's gifts – including an expensive ring – she was even more misguided in confiding in Cathy Bradford. Polly's problem was that she saw good in everyone. If Cathy had stalked the streets by night wielding a blood-stained axe, Polly would have told everyone that there was a perfectly reasonable explanation for her behaviour.

Knowing full well that Owen wanted to commit suicide, Polly unwittingly handed him the very syringe with which he intended to perform the job. When his body was found, she confessed her involvement to Cathy who characteristically advised her to lie through her teeth.

Convinced that Cathy was acting in her best interests, Polly continued to withhold the truth but matters took a turn for the worse when the dead doctor's nephew Josh accused Polly of being a gold-digger and of having a hand in Owen Preston's death. The next thing she knew, Polly was being charged with murder. At her trial Polly finally saw Cathy in her true colours. Not only had she stolen Polly's boyfriend Max – to whom she was now engaged – but in the witness-box, she twisted the truth to make Polly appear guilty. When Polly herself gave evidence, she merely succeeded in digging herself a deeper hole. The verdict was a formality: guilty. The following day, Cathy Bradford, revelling in the media spotlight,

Robbie Cryer needs medical attention after a visit from Cathy Bradford.

appeared on GMTV where, playing the role of the betrayed friend, she seized the opportunity to blacken Polly's name.

A Hostage Situation

Despite a welcome-to-Sun Hill bonk with new DC Rob Thatcher in the interview room, Cathy Bradford still hankered after Brandon Kane, particularly now that he was single following his wife Tanya's mysterious death. So it was eating her up to see him growing closer to PC Honey Harman, and when she discovered that Honey had moved in with Brandon (even though the arrangement was purely platonic), she reacted in typically manic fashion by setting fire to his house. With Brandon and his kids now homeless, Cathy generously allowed them to stay with her. Just when she thought she had got Brandon where she wanted him, he announced that he was moving out. In fury, she viciously attacked her gullible fiancé at his fish and chip shop, bludgeoning Max over the head with her ASP baton before dumping the body in the deep freeze. When the crime was discovered, Cathy was once again a picture of wounded innocence.

However, having found a video at Cathy's house showing CCTV footage from the car park on the night of Tanya's fall, Kane had become suspicious. He began snooping around and enlisted the help of Robbie Cryer who, although no longer working at Sun Hill, still retained a healthy dislike for PC Bradford. On learning that Brandon had been talking to Robbie, Cathy put two and two together and paid her a visit at work. Lying in wait for her as she went home, Bradford smashed Robbie's head against a brick wall, leaving her unconscious on a patch of waste ground.

Although the net was tightening around her,

Bradford takes Brandon Kane hostage.

Cathy still had a few tricks up her sleeve. She arranged a canal-side rendezvous with Brandon but, cunningly stationing herself on the opposite bank, managed to evade capture. Even when her house was put under surveillance, she succeeded in outwitting Sun Hill's finest and, in a last desperate act, she abducted Brandon's two children from school and went on the run. After running rings around her pursuers, she completed a full circle by holing up with the kids in the last place anyone would look – the Sun Hill boiler room. So incompetent were the investigating officers that she had to resort to leaving clues as to her whereabouts. When it finally dawned on them that the target was under their very noses, Brandon went down to try and secure his children's release. Cathy freed them unharmed but was only too happy to take Brandon in their place. He tried to reason with her but she was beyond help and when he tried to leave, she stabbed him with a knife and set fire to the boiler room. The pair were rescued from the inferno and the deranged Cathy was arrested and placed in a Secure Unit. The whole episode – Tanya's death, Cathy's obsession, his children's abduction – had such a profound effect on Brandon that he decided he no longer wanted to be a police officer and tendered his resignation.

The one piece of good news to emerge from the kidnapping was that Cathy's evidence at Polly's trial was now thoroughly discredited. This helped her win an appeal against her murder conviction and although she was unable to rejoin the force (having assisted a suicide and lied under oath), she did return briefly to Sun Hill to work in CAD. Even then there was no respite from her past as she fell victim to an unscrupulous journalist who splashed her story across his newspaper. The penny finally dropped and Polly realised that she was a mite too trusting.

Nick's Decline

DC Juliet Becker made an instant impact at Sun Hill, catching the eye of both Debbie McAllister and Phil Hunter. Becker was happy to swing both ways, but her activities were cruelly curtailed when she was fatally stabbed in the line of duty.

Phil Hunter enjoyed sailing close to the wind and living up to his reputation as the Sun Hill stud, so it came as a massive blow to his ego when medical tests revealed that he was now firing blanks. But if the strain of he and wife Cindy going through IVF did not unsettle him, the return from months in rehab of his old adversary Nick Klein certainly did. For Nick knew all of Phil's most sordid secrets, not least that he was the father of a two-year-old daughter following an affair with the wife of local gangster Dennis Weaver. If

Weaver found out, Phil feared that he would be swapping his sharp suits for a concrete overcoat.

Nick wasted no time in spilling the beans, first to Cindy and then to Weaver. Phil considered that he had got off lightly in being thrown out by Cindy and merely beaten up by Weaver.

A couple of months later Nick was the only witness to the assassination of a convicted murderer, Brendon Bailey, and the finger of guilt pointed at

Phil Hunter and controversial progeny.

Old adversaries: Phil Hunter and Nick Klein.

Weaver. As he walked home from work one night, Nick was grabbed, taken prisoner and injected with heroin on Weaver's orders. Nevertheless he recovered sufficiently to go ahead with identifying Weaver's henchman as the gunman, forcing an increasingly desperate Weaver to lean on Phil for information as to Nick's whereabouts. Phil passed on the address of the safe house and Nick had to be placed on the witness protection scheme. It was the end of Nick Klein's career at Sun Hill. Phil later shot Weaver dead, claiming self-defence.

Manson's Mission

Phil Hunter's other arch enemy was acting DI Samantha Nixon who had survived lurid tabloid stories about her daughter's father being a notorious juvenile murderer to place a strong claim to land the post on a permanent basis. Never lacking in confidence, Samantha was certain that the promotion was hers, only to be overlooked in favour of Neil Manson, a thirty-something high-flier who just happened to be the son-in-law of Deputy Assistant Commissioner Roy Pearson.

Phil's delight at seeing Samantha slapped down was compounded by the fact that he and Manson were at Hendon together and were colleagues as PCs. However he quickly realised that Manson the ambitious DI was a different person to Manson the young copper. This Manson was decidedly taciturn. He was not interested in bonding with the relief and was driven by the need for results rather than making friends.

He was particularly hard on Jack Meadows and, sensing that Jack was approaching his sell-by date, sought to undermine him at every opportunity by going over his head to Okaro while carefully watching

DI Manson was driven by the need for results, not by making friends at Sun Hill.

his own back when rumours spread that his father-in-law was using rent boys. But it wasn't just Jack, Manson also seemed to have a particular problem with female officers, treating Sam with disdain, and hounding Eva Sharpe at every opportunity. He left Eva in no doubt that he wanted her out of Sun Hill and hastily arranged her transfer, only for Jack (with a little help from Mickey Webb) to land her a plum job at MIT.

However, for all Manson's faults, he would not tolerate corruption and was prepared to deal with none other than Don Beech in an attempt to nail Peter Cavanaugh, an Australian detective on attachment to the National Criminal Intelligence Service.

Des Taviner Returns

Although it was widely assumed that Des Taviner had died in the warehouse, the absence of a body meant that there was a distinct possibility that he was still out there somewhere, plotting his next move. Meanwhile Sheelagh Murphy was left with the task of raising Des's daughter, Niamh. One night, shortly after returning to work, Sheelagh caught a glimpse of Taviner lurking in the shadows, but he vanished as quickly as he had appeared.

Tragedy struck when Sheelagh enlisted the help of Aussie PC Cameron Tait for babysitting duties. When Cameron went to check on Niamh, he was horrified to find that the baby had stopped breathing.

Despite his frantic attempts to resuscitate her, she was pronounced dead at St. Hugh's. While a distraught Cameron sought solace in the arms of Kerry Young, Sheelagh tried to come to terms with her loss. The post mortem revealed that neither she nor Cameron were to blame in any way as, unbeknown to them, Niamh had a tiny hole in her heart.

Still reeling from this news, Sheelagh received a visit from Des who was shocked to hear that their baby had died. As the whole relief learned that Des was responsible for the Sun Hill fire, he turned up at the Chapel of Rest to say goodbye to Niamh and persuaded Reg Hollis not to turn him in. CID mounted an 'obbo' at the baby's funeral in the belief that he would show his face again but the wily Des managed to remain at liberty. Hell bent on blaming someone for the death, he took Cameron hostage and threatened to kill him. Cameron bravely talked his way out of the situation and convinced Des that the baby's death was an accident. Cameron was eventually rescued by Kerry who joined him for an emotional reunion in the station shower, no doubt leaving him grateful that he hadn't been rescued by Tony Stamp…

Des then turned his attention to Reg and tried to apologise for everything he had done. Before finishing his speech, however, he was arrested and thrown in a cell with an apparently harmless vagrant, Robert McClusky. Des kept calling for Sheelagh, who was on duty as Custody Sergeant, but she ignored him. Later he was found lying dead in the cell. McClusky had killed him because he wouldn't shut up. Sheelagh was subsequently cleared of negligence but her reputation as a reliable police officer had taken another blow.

While stringing Cameron along, Kerry was playing with fire by having sex with Smithy. More alarmingly,

Gabriel Kent saw an opportunity to exercise his control over her and convinced her that Smithy had date raped her. Cameron supported her all the way, only to be deeply hurt by her betrayal when she decided to withdraw her rape complaint. Gabriel continued to poison Kerry's mind for his own ends until she finally saw through him. Bitter at her rejection and at the news that she was getting engaged to Cameron after all, Gabriel enacted a terrible revenge by raping her. When Kerry looked for backing from her fiancé, she found that Gabriel had managed to convince him that she was nothing more than a slag who cried rape at every opportunity. Even by Sun Hill standards, Gabriel Kent had a lot to answer for.

Taviner is found dead in his cell.

SUN HILL'S YOUNG GUNS

He says: 'When I arrived for fittings at *The Bill* studios and tried on my police uniform, with my blond hair I looked like a male stripper.'

One more thing: Daniel has brains as well as brawn. A MENSA test put him in the top one per cent of Australians.

Last word: 'My very first shot on *The Bill* I was buck-naked. And England is a very cold country compared to Australia!'

BETH CORDINGLY

Alias: PC Kerry Ashton

Age: 26

Previous: Sara Warrington in *Family Affairs* – a hard-drinking, coke-taking lap dancer.

Brush with the law: 'The only naughty thing I did was get into a 15 film when I was 12. It was a fluffy

DANIEL MACPHERSON

Alias: PC Cameron Tait

Age: 23

Previous: As *Neighbours* hunk Joel Samuels, Daniel had an on-screen romance with Holly Valance and was twice voted Australia's Prince of Soap.

Brush with the law: Daniel researched the part with Bondi police, 'cruising around in a squad car, talking to them about what life would be like for Cameron in Sydney. It helped me prepare for the shock he got when he arrived at Sun Hill and ended up walking the beat in the East End.'

On his character: 'He's a good guy but he has a hard edge.'

romantic comedy, but I was just terrified the police were about to burst in and arrest me.' More seriously, Beth had to call in the real police after being stalked by a lovesick fan.

On her character: 'Kerry is lovely but doesn't look before she leaps.'

She says: 'I think the idea of me being a sex kitten is a bit of a joke. I've got a wonky mouth, which is fine, but at drama school they used to tell me I looked like I'd had a stroke.'

One more thing: Beth is no dumb blonde. She has a first class degree in English and drama from Birmingham University.

Last word: Her dad David is a world expert on pirates.

SCOTT NEAL
Alias: PC Luke Ashton

Age: 25

Previous: Trained at the Anna Scher Theatre School, where classmates included former EastEnder Patsy Palmer. He has appeared in *The Knock*, *London's Burning*, cult gay film *Beautiful Thing*.

On his character: 'I've been very lucky. I still can't believe I came across as a convincing police officer. I'm too small, don't look right, done up like a 12-year-old in fancy dress. But you know, I got paid for it.'

He says: 'The uniform gives you a very strange sense of power, but it's totally unflattering. The belt is one of the heaviest things I've ever worn and I don't even dare tell you what I think about the hat!'

One more thing: Although once asked to judge the Mr Gay UK contest in Birmingham, Scott is straight.

Last word: Scott once won £1,500 on a roulette table in Las Vegas.

CIARAN GRIFFITHS
Alias: PC Gary Best
Age: 21
Previous: *Emmerdale*, *Where The Heart Is*, and with Robert Carlyle in the football film *There's Only One Jimmy Grimble*. Most notoriously Ciaran played *Coronation Street*'s Dean Sykes, who was killed holding up a supermarket.

Brush with the law: Since moving to London from Manchester, Ciaran has picked up a stack of parking tickets because he didn't know he needed a residents' permit to park outside his flat.

On his character: 'He's a cocky northern lad with a lot to learn.'

He says: 'When I auditioned for *The Bill* I missed my train and ended up sprinting all the way to the studios from the station. I arrived puffing and sweating so they told me to sit down and take a breather. I found out later that day that I'd got the part.'

One more thing: Ciaran once trained as a hairdresser in Manchester. 'I used to do my mum's hair colouring for her.'

Last word: 'When I was in the series *Children's Ward* I had to do a scene where I streaked clutching two bedpans. The whole cast and crew were there so I was being watched from all angles!'

KIM TIDDY

Alias: PC Honey Harman

Age: 25

Previous: Kim's first role was at school as an Irish Angel Gabriel! 'The teacher wanted Gabriel to be Irish and told me to put on an Irish accent. Goodness knows what I sounded like!'

Brush with the law: Kim received her first parking ticket shortly after joining *The Bill*.

On her character: 'Honey is a breath of fresh air at Sun Hill. Although she may not be the most academically gifted officer, her instinct and physical ability never let her down.'

She says: 'The night before I learned I'd got the role in *The Bill*, I drunkenly walked into a door and bashed my head. I was so happy when my agent called the next morning that I ran up the High Street to find someone I knew to tell them the good news and they thought something awful had happened when they saw me all bloodshot and bruised.'

One more thing: After drama school, Kim ran her own house-cleaning service. 'But I closed the business when I almost wrecked a customer's home.'

Last word: Kim played basketball for England Ladies. 'I was offered a scholarship to go to the United States to do basketball but I chose drama school in Manchester instead.'

CELEBRITY SIGHTINGS

The quality of its hard-hitting storylines has enabled *The Bill* to attract a number of famous faces over the past 20 years, ranging from Lily Savage to footballer Emmanuel Petit. Astute casting has also thrown up several actors who, after minor roles in *The Bill*, have gone on to become household names. Where else would you find a Spice Girl rubbing shoulders with Robert Carlyle?

Here are some of those who have passed through the doors of Sun Hill:

- *Tony Blackburn* appeared as himself to host a quiz in the 2001 episode 'Night Games'.
- Before joining The Spice Girls, *Emma Bunton (Baby Spice)* played troubled teenager Janice in the 1993 episode 'Missionary Work'.
- *Kathy Burke* played a shop assistant who had the misfortune to be locked in a cold store with Reg Hollis in the 1991 episode 'The Negotiator'.
- One of *Robert Carlyle*'s early roles was as a news hack in the 1991 episode 'The Better Part of Valour'.
- A young *Michelle Collins* played a teenage tearaway in 1986.
- In 1999 *Roger Daltrey* played former jailbird Larry Moore, who, fearing another spell in prison, shot his daughter and then himself.
- Taking a break from Albert Square, *Letitia Dean* played suspected arsonist Amanda Ronson in 1997.
- *Fish*, the former singer with Marillion, played David Lewson in a 1998 episode 'Manhunt'.
- Before appearing as Robbie Jackson in *Eastenders*, *Dean Gaffney* played 13-year-old drugs courier Terry Jakes in a 1992 episode of *The Bill*.

A young Michelle Collins as a troubled tee

An undercover Alex Kingston takes Matt Boyden's fancy.

Chesney Hawkes is arrested.

Martin Kemp threatens Reg Hollis.

- *Leslie Grantham* starred as ruthless gangster Jimmy Smith in the 1998 story 'The Personal Touch'.
- *Chesney Hawkes* played a character called Colin who was arrested for drug dealing in the March 1991 episode 'Photo Finish'.
- *Martin Kemp* held Reg Hollis hostage as gunman Tom Marsh in the 1998 story 'The Bus Driver's Prayer'.
- *Alex Kingston* of *ER* fame played DS Lisa Holm, who posed undercover as high-class hooker 'Lisa Royle' in an April 1995 episode 'In on the Game'.
- *Hugh Laurie* kept a straight face as defence counsel Harrap in the three-part story 'Good Faith' (1998)
- *Linda Lusardi* played Don Beech's girlfriend Maggie Lyons in the 2000 episode 'The River'.

- *Rik Mayall* appeared as evil gambler Patrick Massie, who was arrested for deliberately pushing his 16-year-old son Jimmy from a high building in 1997.
- In her pre-Bianca days, *Patsy Palmer* played Suzanne in the 1991 story 'Shots'.
- France and Arsenal midfielder *Emmanuel Petit* guested as himself, visiting a hospitalised girl in the 1998 Christmas episode.
- *Lily Savage (aka Paul O'Grady)* first appeared as Ted Roach's transvestite snout Roxanne in 1990.
- *Eric Sykes* made a guest appearance in 2003 as Ted, a confused pensioner.
- *Denise Van Outen* played gangster's moll Melanie Lehmann in the 1998 episode 'The Personal Touch'.

Tony Stamp can smell Fish.

Dean Gaffney tries to look well 'ard.

Roger Daltrey appeared as an ex-con in 1999 alongside Don Beech (Billy Murray).

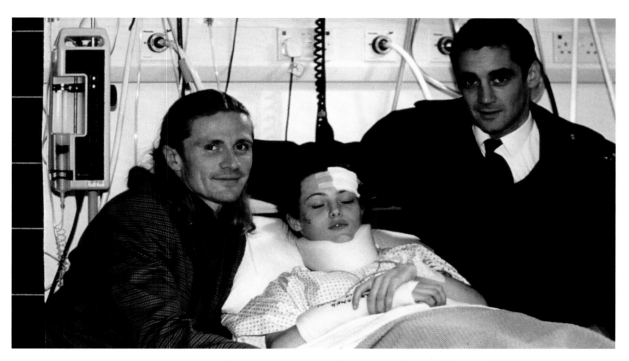

Footballer Emmanuel Petit played himself in the 1998 Christmas episode.

BLASTS AND BRAWLS

Even by Sun Hill standards, it was quite an explosion. The firebomb blast that destroyed the station – and six officers – in April 2002 was the most spectacular stunt in the history of *The Bill*.

Special effects expert Neal Champion and his team planned the blast like a military operation over a number of months. They began by fireproofing a condemned building to contain the heat and then they removed all the glass from the windows, replacing it with sheets of a special resin that shatters like glass but doesn't cut. Finally, no fewer than 60 separate explosions of gunpowder, petrol and gas were triggered simultaneously to create the fireball effect.

'Of course, we only had one take,' said Champion, 'so the pressure was on. Happily it all went off perfectly.'

Graham Cole (aka Tony Stamp) prides himself on never having had to use a stunt double on *The Bill*. He says: 'I get a real adrenalin buzz from doing the driving stunts but it's a huge responsibility. There'll be Reg (Hollis) or Dave (Quinnan) in the passenger seat, usually a prisoner in the back, along with the lighting director, a sound man and sometimes the director. So that's five more lives in the car to worry about, plus a £36,000 camera strapped to the door, and you're told to go round the Elephant and Castle as fast as you can – and remember your lines.

'I call the people who have to sit beside me the white-knuckle brigade, and Andy Paul (who played Dave Quinnan) is the president…still. He hated all that stuff.

'I've had lots of hairy moments and I've been hospitalised about ten times, usually cuts and bruises from breaking into buildings or doing fight scenes. You often get an elbow in the eye or a knee in the groin. With just one hand-held camera, you have to make it look good.'

Graham Cole gets a buzz from driving stunts.

The Sun Hill bomb blast was staged with military precision.

Conway's car goes up in flames.

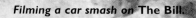

Filming a car smash on The Bill.

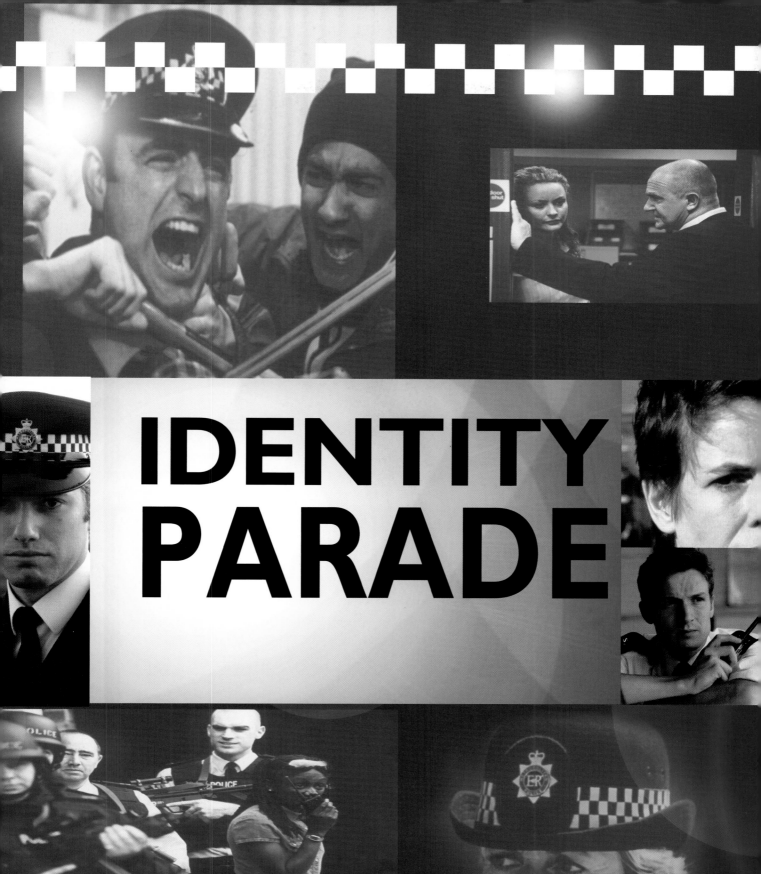

IDENTITY
PARADE

PC Timothy Able.

PC Timothy Able
(Mark Haddigan) (1989)
The youngest of three brothers (his mother worked in a sportswear shop, his father was a train driver), Londoner Able joined Sun Hill as a probationer. Although he excelled at the physical side of the job, he failed to live up to his name when it came to taking statements and conducting interviews, a state of affairs that brought him into conflict with Inspector Christine Frazer, who ordered him to undergo additional training in both. Failed to make the grade.

PC/Sgt. June Ackland
(Trudie Goodwin) (1983–present)
The saintly June has been married to Sun Hill for longer than she'd care to remember. Apart from a brief fling with DCI Wray, she was a paragon of virtue until getting together with Jim Carver in a meeting of two lonely souls, a relationship that ultimately turned sour. June has always managed to keep her cool while all around were losing theirs, a rare lapse occurring after the death of her invalid father, for whom she had lovingly cared for many years. The loss hit her so badly that she was discovered drunk on duty and was packed off to a sauna to sober up. More popular with her colleagues than she probably thinks, her promotion to sergeant was richly deserved. In 2002 she was appointed head of the Community Safety Unit.

PC Luke Ashton
(Scott Neal) (1997–9, 2002–3)
Baby-faced Ashton first came to Sun Hill as a naïve probationer fresh from Hendon. Puppy-walked by Tony Stamp, he endured a baptism of fire, watching a young lad plunge to his death from a rooftop. When a hostage situation ended in tragedy, leaving two people dead, Ashton decided he was in the wrong job and went backpacking to distant lands. He returned three years later more confident of his own abilities, only to fall victim to the predatory Craig Gilmore. Despite being caught in bed with his sergeant on the morning of his wedding, Ashton went on to marry PC Kerry Young but their relationship foundered when the truth about his sexuality emerged and he left Sun Hill soon afterwards.

DC Juliet Becker
(Rae Baker, 2003)
The daughter of a military chaplain, motorbike-riding Juliet is more than just a pretty face. Self-assured, professional and diplomatic, she liked to keep her work and private life very separate. Happily single, she has a relaxed attitude to sex, which she saw as a fun activity, and was attracted to people rather than gender, although she hated the term 'bi-sexual'. After just a few months at Sun Hill, she was fatally stabbed in the line of duty.

DS Don Beech
(Billy Murray) (1995–2000, 2004)
The bad apple that upset the Sun Hill cart. He was a maverick, a loose cannon, a gambler, who thought that rules were only for bending, but even his biggest enemy had to admit grudgingly that he got results. As John Boulton discovered to his cost, he was a dangerous adversary, one who was equally adept at sweet-talking beautiful women and senior officers. He had a long-standing girlfriend, Maggie, and could charm the leaves from the trees but would probably only

SUN HILL – *The Facts*
Not counting walk-ons, over 8,500 actors have appeared in The Bill in the course of its 20-year run.

bother if he could obtain a good price for them. He took more backhanders than Tim Henman and when the net closed in, he fled to Australia and embarked on a spree of bank robberies before faking his own death. Returning to England, he was finally brought to justice by Claire Stanton, Boulton's former lover, but even as he was led off to prison he vowed that he would be free in a year. You just can't keep a bad man down.

PC Gary Best

(Ciaran Griffiths) (2002–present)
If you gave Gary a penny for his thoughts, you'd get change. It's not that he's stupid, he's just a bit slow on the uptake and definitely not one of life's great philosophers. He thinks Freud is a prefix of bacon. Raised on the mean streets of Manchester where most of his old schoolmates are guests of Her Majesty, he knows that if he weren't in a uniform, he'd be in prison. He chose the police partly as a way of sticking two fingers up at his bullying father, who used to beat him black and blue until he was big enough to fight back. Gary also has a tendency to rush around like a headless chicken, an attitude that causes him to regard Tony Stamp as a living, breathing Mr Plod. Gary breaks life down into four manageable compartments – women, football, lager and the job – in that order.

PC Jamila Blake

(Lolita Chakrabarti) (1996–8)

If Jamila were ever the life and soul of the party, it would be a party to avoid at all costs. Dour, dedicated and with what seemed to be a permanent chip on her shoulder, she could never be accused of putting the 'sun' into Sun Hill. Although her intimidating nature struck fear into suspects and colleagues alike, she did have her admirers. When she walked up the ramp into Sun Hill wearing a suit for her attachment to CID, Nick Slater and Tony Stamp commented that a body like hers definitely belonged in a uniform. Some may have thought a suit of armour more appropriate.

PC Adam Bostock

(Carl Brincat) (1994)
A flash young officer who was transferred from 4 Area after falling out with his previous governor. Although only three years out of probation, Bostock thought he knew it all and intended to enjoy life to the max. He was in for a rude awakening and did not last long at Sun Hill.

DS John Boulton

(Russell Boulter) (1995–2000)
Nicknamed 'Robocop' by his colleagues, Boulton was desperate to be top dog in CID and would go to any lengths to secure a conviction, seeing himself as Sun Hill's one-man vigilante force. At

PC Jamila Blake.

times his zeal for nicking criminals bordered on the psychotic and he was not averse to roughing up suspects either to make them more talkative or simply as an act of vengeance. Whilst he was unpopular with Uniform and most of CID, his combination of obsession and aggression proved strangely attractive to women, notably Claire Stanton, with whom he broke the habit of a lifetime by sharing information as well as bodily fluids. Whenever Boulton got a lead, he was like a terrier with a bone but sadly this approach brought him into conflict with a rottweiller in the shape of Don Beech and he received a fatal blow to the head for his trouble.

Sgt. Matthew Boyden

(Tony O'Callaghan) (1991–2003)
Matt Boyden's eye didn't just rove, it ran marathons. The officer with a girl in every station developed his smooth patter while working on Margate funfairs as a boy. After leaving a clerical job with British Rail to join the Met, he passed his sergeant's exams in 1985, but being caught 'over the side' with a WPC probationer at his sergeant's course in Hendon effectively ended his marriage and his chances of future promotion. A further indiscretion with a WDC at Romford necessitated his move to Sun Hill, where he arrived with more baggage than Judith Chalmers. Although the clean shirt in his locker, plus toothbrush, toothpaste and electric razor in his drawer indicated his true priorities, he came across as a caring, compassionate sergeant who was well liked by most of the Relief. He often sailed close to the wind – witness his association with an under-age girl in 1999, his affair with Vicky Hagen and his fling with Sam Nixon's 15-year-old daughter Abigail. Let's just say that whilst Boyden was popular in some quarters, there was no shortage of suspects when he was murdered.

PC Cathy Bradford

(Connie Hyde) (2002–4)
An inspector with the Hong Kong police for six years before coming to Sun Hill, Bradford is Sun Hill's resident psychopath. For although outwardly ambitious and self-confident, she is mentally unstable. She saw joining June Ackland's Community Safety Unit as a first step towards regaining her former rank but the CSU proved to be the worst placement imaginable for a lying, racist, homophobic, homicidal, back-stabbing bunny boiler. As Jim Carver remarked: 'Bradford? She's got about as much community spirit as Adolf Hitler!' She then developed a fatal attraction to married DC Brandon Kane and was prepared to threaten – or even kill – anybody who came between them.

PC Claire Brind

(Kelly Lawrence) (1988–9)
The well-meaning but accident-prone daughter of a former DI, young Brind was never really cut out for the force. The butt of jokes both in the station and on the streets, she struggled to assert her authority and disliked certain aspects of the job. When asked to play a missing girl for a TV reconstruction, she complained about the high-heeled shoes she had to wear, saying they had threatened her ability to have children. Although she occasionally showed commendable initiative,

her moaning and poor timekeeping did not exactly endear her to her sergeants. Her finest moment was dressing up as a kissogram for 'Yorkie' Smith's leaving party.

Chief Supt. Charles Brownlow

(Peter Ellis) (1984–2000)
All image but very little substance, Brownlow was the ultimate politician whose worst nightmare was negative publicity. Shielded from the outside world by his long-suffering secretary Marion, he unquestioningly obeyed every directive from the commissioner's office, regardless of whether or not it was practical or even desirable.

PC Claire Brind.

SUN HILL – The Facts

Connie Hyde (PC Cathy Bradford) had previously appeared on
The Bill *first as a computer expert and then as a prostitute.*
She says: 'I was working in a brothel and dodgy detective
DS Beech flashed his bottom at me!'

So terrified was he of antagonising the local communities that he effectively shackled his own officers and lived in dread of mavericks such as Burnside bringing Sun Hill into disrepute. As he became increasingly out of touch with those at the sharp end, he began to lose their confidence and respect. His fondness of the empty gesture was perfectly illustrated when he decided to eat in the canteen with the other ranks to show that he was a man of the people. It was an excruciating experience for his staff although Brownlow, never able to admit to a mistake, considered it to have been a valuable exercise in public relations. For all his faults he was essentially a decent, if somewhat blinkered, man and it was difficult not to feel some sympathy for him when he felt obliged to tender his resignation in the wake of the Don Beech corruption scandal that engulfed Sun Hill.

DS/DI/DCI Frank Burnside

(Christopher Ellison) (1984, 1986, 1988–93, 1998–2000)

'Sharp' is the word that springs to mind when describing Frank Burnside. Sharp features, sharp mind, sharp tongue, sharp practice. Sun Hill's man of mystery first appeared in 1984 as a DS from another station. Everyone thought he was bent, but nobody dared accuse him to his face. Promoted to DI, he became Sun Hill's arch thief-taker famous for his colourful turn of phrase, the Burnside glare and a penchant for shoving suspects' heads down toilets by way of encouraging confession. Steely and uncompromising, he was not a man to cross. He could be fiercely loyal to his colleagues – when it suited him – and although essentially a loner since his divorce, he had no shortage of female admirers. Many superior officers tried to tame him but none succeeded. Burnside simply became more devious. His talents did not go unnoticed from above and a further promotion accompanied a prolonged spell of dangerous undercover work. He then joined the elite National Crime Squad, where he was able to do what he did best – nick villains.

PC Ruby Buxton

(Nicola Alexis) (2002–2003)
Local girl Ruby left school at the age of 18 and, tired of studying, ended up working in a shop. But she soon developed itchy feet and was attracted by the Met's recruitment drive, reasoning that 26 grand a year and free travel was a tastier proposition than the checkout at the supermarket. Easygoing, vivacious and bubbly, she quickly settled into life at Sun Hill, much to the amusement of her mates who give her stick when she's out on the beat.

PC/DC Jim Carver

(Mark Wingett) (1983–present)
Earnest, intense and scrupulously honest, Jim Carver had all the makings of a first-class sergeant in the Bob Cryer mould. Instead he allowed himself to be seduced by the bright lights of CID where, despite occasionally allowing his heart to rule his head, he developed into a reliable, if unspectacular, performer who was not afraid to suffer pain in the line of duty. His antipathy towards some of Burnside's more dubious working practices was offset by Frank's charisma but after his mentor left Sun Hill, Carver's career drifted into decline, culminating in his being switched back to Uniform as part of the policy of Tenure. Although the move was standard procedure,

SUN HILL – The Facts

Two years after filming a guest spot on **The Bill** *as a getaway driver, Tony O'Callaghan was offered the role of Sgt. Matt Boyden. He claimed he was told he would earn a regular slot in the show by a clairvoyant in a hairdresser's!*

Carver took it as a slight on his ability and began hitting the bottle with a vengeance. When June Ackland rallied round to help him overcome his alcoholism, Carver began to see her in a new light and before long they had moved in together. But in the end he went off and married a woman he had met through his role as Family Liaison Officer and who understood his problems. He almost had something to smile about.

Chief Insp. Philip Cato

(Philip Whitchurch) (1992–5)
'The bald-headed bastard from Barton Street', as Burnside called him, ruffled more feathers than a fox in a henhouse. He did not suffer fools (or anyone for that matter), especially those whom he perceived as being unsympathetic to his methods, which owed much to the Genghis Khan school of policing. Although in private he would admit to a dislike of petty bureaucracy, his hypocrisy and sense of self-preservation ensured that such views were never aired within Brownlow's earshot. Initially Brownlow welcomed Cato as someone even less popular than himself with the troops but soon he realised that the new man's radical approach was having an adverse effect on station morale. Consequently Brownlow was privately relieved to hear that Cato had resigned in a fit of pique after a

Chief Insp. Philip Cato.

failed application for an Acting promotion.

Supt. Tom Chandler

(Steven Hartley) (2000–2)
Sexy, well-educated, charis-matic and politically astute, Chandler represented the new, firm but caring, acceptably liberal face of the Met. as it sought to claw back some credibility and restore the shine on its tarnished image. He was seen by Borough Commander Guy Mannion as the ideal man to revitalise Sun Hill but his gung-ho pursuit of high-profile policies threatened to undermine others' good work, while the adrenalin of power fuelled his Clintonesque weakness around women. Soon his dark past

began to catch up with him. A rape allegation from his Hendon days emerged, and not even marriage to DS Debbie McAllister could halt his downward spiral. Backed into a corner by the dogged investigation of Meadows and Webb, he decided that the only way out was to take his own life.

PC Roz Clarke

(Holly Davidson) (2000–1)
Roz joined Sun Hill at the same time as fellow probationer Ben Hayward but struggled to make ends meet financially. Unable to secure enough overtime to pay her debts, she moon-lighted in telesales, as a result of which her police work suffered. When she failed her exams, she considered leaving the force but got a second chance to prove her worth in CID. However, she couldn't handle the pressure after being attacked by a potential rapist and decided that her future lay elsewhere.

Chief Insp. Derek Conway

(Ben Roberts) (1988–2002)
An old-fashioned copper, Conway hid a laconic sense of humour behind a gruff exterior. Despite his elevated rank (he always suspected that Brownlow blocked further progress), he believed that real police work took place on the streets rather than in meeting rooms and had little time for new

initiatives and modern theories. And when he did come up with a scheme, it invariably backfired. Seeking to stamp out the drinking culture at Sun Hill, he was caught searching Christine Frazer's filing cabinet and was found in possession of a pair of her knickers! A skilful negotiator who was surprisingly successful in his stint as Community Liaison Officer, he was killed by a car bomb at the height of the area's racist wars. He left behind a wife and three children.

DC Suzi Croft

(Kerry Peers) (1993–8)

As a trainee investigator, Welsh-born Croft was the dogsbody of CID. She faced a constant battle to make herself heard in that chauvinistic world, often finding herself assigned to menial duties while the boys were out playing cops and robbers. However, she gradually proved herself to be an intelligent, thoughtful detective – in sharp contrast to the Neanderthal Rod Skase – her skills considerably enhanced by attending a special interviewing course run by the Met. In 1998 she transferred to High Barnet to be near her boyfriend.

Sgt. Bob Cryer

(Eric Richard) (1984–2001)

Firm but fair with a wealth of experience and an unshakeable moral code, Bob Cryer's belief in discipline tempered by pragmatism

DC Suzi Croft.

stemmed from his army days. Married with two children (his son Patrick was once charged with causing a girl's death by dangerous driving), he also acted as a father figure to new recruits at Sun Hill. He was promoted to duty sergeant in 1991 and although he never harboured any great ambitions, as the years passed he began to feel stuck in a rut, becoming less tolerant of inept young constables, particularly those who did not take the job seriously enough. Ever since shooting dead an armed robber (whose gun turned out not to be loaded), Bob was uneasy about firearms and they returned to haunt him when he was accidentally shot in the side by PC Dale Smith after being taken hostage at a school. Ironically it was Cryer who had pushed Smith to join SO19. Initially confined to a wheelchair, Cryer was told by Ackland that he was not expected to return to Sun Hill. Typically, at his leaving do, he sought out Smith to offer words of reassurance.

Front Desk Officer Roberta Cryer

(Moya Brady) (2002–3)

When a new front desk officer arrived at Sun Hill, those with a nose for intrigue couldn't help thinking there was something strangely familiar about her. It turned out that she was Bob Cryer's niece, Roberta. Raised by foster parents in Blackpool, the vivacious Robbie came to London in 2001 and landed a job as a receptionist at a toilet roll factory. Then, on the recommendation of Uncle Bob, she applied for the civvy job at Sun Hill. A compulsive gossip with a string of boyfriends, she has been a welcome addition to the station's social scene while nursing a broken heart for the departing Mickey Webb.

DI Alex Cullen
(Ged Simmons) (2000–2)
Cullen was always viewed with suspicion by the rest of CID as being Tom Chandler's man. Chandler's only direct appointment, Cullen was a no-nonsense, slightly taciturn individual who acted as the superintendent's unofficial hatchet man. However when the two became involved in a power struggle, Cullen applied for a transfer to MIT. Unwilling to let him go, Chandler thought about blocking the move but Cullen's knowledge of past dirty laundry saw the transfer completed within days. At Sun Hill it's not only who you know but what you know.

DS Geoff Daly
(Ray Ashcroft) (1996–2000)
A phlegmatic Yorkshireman with a wry sense of humour, Daly was handpicked by Deakin to join the CID team on account of his considerable experience in all areas of crime. He specialised in child protection but made it his business to be *au fait* with modern developments in every aspect of the job. Nobody's fool, Daly quickly had the measure of Skase and Boulton and was the first to become suspicious of Beech, with whom he tangled on a number of occasions. His in-stincts were proved correct, al-though ironically he was one of two CID officers ordered to be transferred from Sun Hill after Beech's corruption was finally revealed.

DC Mike Dashwood
(Jon Iles) (1984–92)
A bit of a poser was Mike. Suave and sophisticated with a private income that enabled him to swan off to the country at weekends, he was more likely to socialise with lords of the manor than with Ted Roach. Since there was a feeling that he tended to look down on some of his CID colleagues, they took great delight whenever he screwed up, which was by no means a rare occurrence. However, he gradually won their respect ,before leaving to accept a more suitable position with Scotland Yard's Art and Antiques Squad.

PC Norika Datta
(Seeta Indrani) (1989–98)
Norika's parents were Kenyan

PC Roz Clarke.

SUN HILL – The Facts

Before becoming an actor, Shaun Scott (DI Chris Deakin) went for an interview with Surrey Police.

Asians who ran a shop in Uxbridge and she worked as junior in a hairdresser's before joining the police. At Sun Hill her calm efficiency and pleasing smile won her a host of admirers, but she didn't believe in mixing business with pleasure (her white boyfriend Peter was a sports teacher). This didn't stop Jim Carver trying his luck nor, more sinisterly, Phil Young, who sexually assaulted her in a terrifying ordeal. In 1993 Norika began working with the Domestic Violence Unit and found the work so rewarding that when she left Sun Hill it was to join the Crime Policy Unit, developing guidelines on domestic violence.

DS/DI Chris Deakin

(Shaun Scott) (1994–2000)
Busted down from DI in the Flying Squad after having an affair with a senior officer's wife, Deakin sought to resurrect his career at Sun Hill but found his path blocked by Sally Johnson. Never keen on women superiors, Deakin succeeded in undermining her and quickly stepped into her shoes when she left. Deakin was a respected thief-taker who exuded an air of quiet menace. While willing to cut corners if necessary, he was in no way bent, but unfortunately for him this did not apply to everyone at Sun Hill. While

Deakin was busy turning a blind eye, Don Beech was wreaking havoc. Deakin finally paid for his inactivity with another kick in the career teeth.

DS Ramani De Costa

(Thusitha Jayasundera)
(2003–present)
With a computer-like brain that is prone to crashing occasionally and surrounded by what she likes to call organised chaos, De Costa comes across as the archetypal mad professor. But her engaging personality and background in sexual offences training quickly made her an invaluable member of the CSU, and when Ackland stepped down as its head, she recommended De Costa as her successor.

DC Ken Drummond

(Russell Floyd) (2002–present)
A father of six (he's a lapsed Catholic but some rules still apply), Drummond has spent most of his career with his feet up on the desk. The only time he breaks into a sweat is at the prospect of food. Indeed his closest friends in the station are the canteen staff, who always give him preferential treatment, to the chagrin of Reg Hollis, who has campaigned for years for poached eggs on toast.

PC Norika Datta.

DC Ken Drummond.

abandoned in the street by his mates from Sun Hill, much to the annoyance of Mary, his Welsh bride-to-be. After brushes with pigs, chickens and assorted oddballs, he asked for a transfer back to Wales. His final day convinced him he had made the right decision: Brownlow didn't seem to know who he was and Conway thought he'd already left. In the end he decided to give his own leaving a party a miss and headed home alone.

PC Suzanne Ford
(Vikki Gee-Dare) (1989–91)
Caring Suzanne Ford considered becoming a nurse before joining the police and saw her role as serving the community rather than catching criminals. As she had a profoundly deaf sister, she was able to use sign language and thus became an invaluable member of the Sun Hill team.

Occasionally, when roused, Drummond will bring in a good collar and indeed his colleagues defend him to the hilt to outsiders. He may be a lazy bastard, but he's *their* lazy bastard. Despite a taste in shirts that would scare horses and which belies the description of 'plainclothes detective', Drummond seemed like an all-round good guy until it emerged that he had been cheating on his wife Fiona. After his marriage fell apart, his son was taken hostage by a gang of carjackers and Drummond, working undercover, was forced to take part in an armed robbery to secure the boy's release. He had finally earned that bacon sandwich.

PC Francis 'Taffy' Edwards
(Colin Blumenau) (1983–1990)
A quiet country boy who hailed from a poor farming family near Bangor, Edwards sometimes struggled to adapt to city life. He got hopelessly drunk on his stag night and ended up stripped naked and

PC Robin Frank
(Ashley Gunstock) (1984–8)
A schoolteacher's son from Bethnal Green, Frank worked in office jobs before joining the Met. Married to Angela, a nurse, he suffered the trauma of being shot by a robber who had taken a woman hostage in a block of flats. Recuperating, Frank spent much of his time at the CAD desk, where he was occasionally ticked off by Ackland for whistling loudly. Luckily it wasn't considered a disciplinary offence.

Insp. Christine Frazer

(Barbara Thorn) (1988–90)

A staunch feminist, Christine Frazer turned up for her first day at Sun Hill in plain clothes and immediately found herself chatted up by Ted Roach in the pub. When Roach discovered who she was, they embarked on a torrid affair that became the talk of the station. She said she was attracted to his wild, sexy ways, which basically meant that she fancied a bit of rough. But she held no such affection for Derek Conway, who was a constant thorn in her side, leading her to present Brownlow with a 'him or me' ultimatum. When Brownlow sided with Conway, Frazer decided to leave Sun Hill and write a thesis on 'Women's Career Patterns in the Force'. Dave Quinnan thought it was something to do with knitting.

PC Delia French

(Natasha Williams) (1990–2)

Once in charge of the station typing pool (where she blasted 'Tosh' Lines for the poor quality of CID tapes presented to her girls for audio-typing), Jamaican-born French left to take a clerical job in the city before returning to Sun Hill as a probationary WPC. Her infectious enthusiasm was soon put to the test when she encountered her first taste of racial hatred on the Jasmine Allen Estate.

DI Roy Galloway

(Robert Pugh/John Salthouse) (1983–7)

Fiery Roy Galloway was proud of being the youngest DI in the division. A hard taskmaster who was not afraid to bend the rules in order to get a result, he never set out to cultivate friendships at Sun Hill. His reluctance to take time off led to domestic friction and he often took out his anger and frustration on those around him at work. Bob Cryer may not have approved of some of Galloway's methods but the two men shared a mutual respect and when Cryer accidentally knocked down and killed an old lady, the DI protected him in the face of the hostile Inspector Kite. Galloway's sudden departure came as a shock to some, a relief to others.

PC George Garfield

(Huw Higginson) (1989–99)

Poor George, he was one of life's losers. People took advantage of his good nature, as a result of which he was frequently at his wits' end, although, to be honest, it wasn't a long journey. Gullible could have been his middle name. Despite being a popular Federation rep, his prospects of making sergeant were hampered by his tendency to behave like a bull in a china shop, perhaps a legacy of his younger days as an amateur boxer. Women seemed allergic to him and when he did finally land a steady girlfriend – Jenny, a nurse – he lost her to Dave Quinnan. That was the last straw for George and, sick of the job

and of life, he decided to leave Sun Hill and go off travelling.

Sgt. Craig Gilmore

(Hywel Simons) (2001–3)

Swansea-born Gilmore came out to his family at the age of 19. Openly gay, he lived with his partner Carl, a computer programmer, but, on arriving at Sun Hill, developed an unhealthy obsession with young PC Luke Ashton. He managed to overcome homophobic jibes from the likes of Matthew Boyden and Des Taviner but Ashton's wedding to Kerry Young was too much for him to

PC Delia French.

take and he requested a transfer, a process that was hastened after he took a severe beating while guarding a suspect.

DC Danny Glaze

(Karl Collins) (1999–2003)
Having arrived at Sun Hill looking like the sixth member of the Jackson Five, Londoner Danny wisely decided that his Afro was hardly ideal for a CID officer wanting to go incognito on the Bronte. His new shaven-headed look has coincided with a maturing approach. Smart, sassy and streetwise, he is definite DS material and showed his sympathetic side when dealing with Sister Sarah whose needle exchange centre had become a haven for drugs. He even resisted the jokes about meeting a nun with a habit. However he was still haunted by his cover-up role in the Sun Hill race wars of 2002 and when details of his involvement began to emerge, he fled to South Africa.

Insp. Gina Gold

(Roberta Taylor) (2002–present)
Chain-smoking Gina Gold has the capacity to terrify every rank of officer when the mood takes her. Best described as 'ballsy', she can be funny, sarcastic and downright rude, all in the space of the same

SUN HILL – The Facts

Actress Roberta Taylor, who plays Inspector Gina Gold, once worked as a dental nurse.

sentence. But behind her super-confident exterior, the bookmaker's daughter hides a secret sadness – her brother Richard committed suicide in jail after being wrongly convicted of murder. Back in the Eighties she and Adam Okaro were lovers, which comes in handy when she needs to put the new superintendent in his place. First in and last to leave, dedicated Gina is always at her post. If not, she's probably in the ladies' lighting up yet another cigarette.

DS Alistair Greig

Andrew Mackintosh) (1989–98)
Intelligent, straight, and blessed with a dry Scottish sense of humour, Greig joined Sun Hill after studying law and then serving with the Vice Squad at West End Central. His clarinet playing may have amused Burnside and Roach but they soon realised that his somewhat prissy attitude belied a shrewd brain. The three were never likely to be drinking buddies, however, as Greig eschewed their corner-cutting and laddish behaviour. He also opted out of roughing up suspects for fear of

getting blood on his suit or, worse still in view of his promotion aspirations, on his hands. He left Sun Hill rather than face a return to Uniform after his appeal against Tenure was rejected.

PC Vicky Hagen

(Samantha Robson) (1998–2001)
The bitch of Sun Hill, Hagen arrived from a nick in Essex with the unwanted reputation of being someone who had grassed on a fellow officer. Those of her new colleagues who were not already prejudiced against her were then swiftly alienated by her abrasive approach. A thinly disguised man-eater (she took naturally to going undercover as a prostitute), Hagen fell for the dubious charms of Eddie Santini before moving on to Matt Boyden. When it became clear that Boyden put his troubled daughter Amy before her, Hagen finally demonstrated signs of vulnerability. On the rebound, she picked up a guy for a one-night stand, only for him to commit suicide in the bath. In the circumstances, she decided it was best to ask Chandler for a transfer.

DI Harry Haines

(Gary Whelan) (1993–4)
Following Burnside's abrupt exit, Haines was transferred to Sun Hill from the Drugs Squad. Built like a

SUN HILL – The Facts

The character of PC Delia French was originally the civilian manager of Sun Hill's typing pool and was billed as Miss France.

SUN HILL – *The Facts*

Huw Higginson, who played PC George Garfield, was once sacked from his job as a labourer for putting his pick through a mains pipe.

prop forward (as befitted a former member of the Divisional rugby team), his easy manner and ironic sense of humour could not disguise the fact that he was a cunning operator and as hard as iron. After just three months, interference from Meadows over the discovery of an LSD factory made him choose to leave Sun Hill and return to the Drugs Squad.

PC Sam Harker
(Matthew Crompton)
(1998–2002)
Hailing from a family of coppers (his father and elder brother were both in the force), the easy-going Scouser joined Sun Hill from Heathrow police in order to broaden his experience. He carried a torch for Cass Rickman but shone it in all the wrong places and she made it clear that they could never be more than friends. Sam died in hospital of a heart attack following the petrol bombing of Sun Hill.

PC Honey Harman
(Kim Tiddy) (2003–present)
'Honey Harman,' sighed Matt Boyden as the new girl blundered into Sun Hill. 'Bit of a bungalow – nothing up top.' Nevertheless Honey quickly had the men swarming around her like bees. A vegetarian who declared her body

to be a temple, she soon found that there was no shortage of worshippers even though she professed to be ignorant of the effect she had on the male species. Born and bred in Ilford, dizzy Honey struggled academically at school but excelled at sport. After working as a fitness instructor and personal trainer, she elected to channel her physical attributes into police work. The only thing she hates about the job is paperwork. Luckily there are plenty of volunteers only too willing to help her...particularly Gary Best.

PC Donna Harris
(Louise Harrison) (1991–6)
A Yorkshire lass, pretty blonde Donna was widowed at the age of 20 when her husband was killed in a car crash. She joined the Met. in 1981 and re-married six years later to an older man who had a daughter from his first marriage. In order to spend more time with her new family, she moved to Sun Hill as a collator, keeping comprehensive files on every known villain in the area.

PC Malcolm Haynes
(Eamonn Walker) (1988–9)
A young black officer stationed at Brixton during the riots in the summer of 1981, Haynes was used

to life on the front line. He undertook dangerous undercover operations at Sun Hill but was shocked by the death of his erstwhile partner, Pete Ramsey, who was shot in the aftermath of a bank raid. Frazer told Haynes that he had the potential to go for sergeant but Haynes wondered whether promotion would simply be an empty gesture as part of the Met.'s black recruitment drive.

PC Donna Harris.

DC Kerry Holmes.

PC Ben Hayward

(Ben Peyton) (2000–2)
Well-educated and confident, Hayward could have gone a long way in the force. Unfortunately his confidence sometimes bordered on arrogance, he had no time for routine police work, which led to accusations of laziness, and for someone with four top grade 'A' Levels he often displayed a distinct lack of commonsense. He had a particular bee in his bonnet about drugs, his sister having died from taking Ecstasy. What should have been a promising career was cut short when he was killed in the explosion that shook the station.

PC Reg Hollis

(Jeff Stewart) (1984–present)
One of life's great moaners, Hollis loves to listen to gossip and is always ready to initiate unwarranted doom and gloom around the station. He is also a confirmed hypochondriac and has suffered every ailment known to man as well as a few that medical science has yet to discover. A loner who spends much of his spare time playing with his model railway, Hollis does have his uses. It was he who revived the station garden and he has a genuine rapport with the vulnerable, the young and the elderly, sometimes to the amusement of his colleagues. They were amazed when he was accused – wrongly as it turned out – of murdering an old lady. He then suffered another trauma, being taken hostage in a disused slaughterhouse. Against all odds, he struck up a bizarre friendship with his 'chalk-and-cheese' patrol partner, Des Taviner, who affectionately christened him 'Reggie Baby'. Not surprisingly, Reg didn't see the irony. When he spent weeks in hospital following Taviner's death, there were even those who grudgingly admitted that they would have been sorry if he hadn't pulled through. That's about as close to station popularity as Reg Hollis is ever likely to get.

DC Kerry Holmes

(Joy Brook) (1998–2000)
Bright, intelligent and highly motivated, Holmes earned the reputation for being a bit of a swot among her younger male colleagues, but she was confident enough to handle their jibes and come back with a quick riposte. She was not afraid to use her femininity when it suited her, one of her most interesting assignments being when she went undercover in a women's prison and found herself naked in the shower with a lesbian inmate. Eighteen months later Kerry requested a transfer from Sun Hill following the Don Beech corruption scandal.

DS Phil Hunter

(Scott Maslen) (2002–present)
After barely surviving the Beech debacle, Jack Meadows needed Phil Hunter like a hole in the head. For Hunter is very much a junior version of Beech – a flash ladies' man who is in the pocket of the local criminal fraternity. Hunter is motivated solely by greed and likes his women to be as fast as his cars. He gets his kicks from living dangerously but sometimes gets out of his depth. Backed into a corner, he can be ruthlessly unscrupulous. He would sell his own wife if he had to – and he has. But Ron Gregory was a villain too far and Hunter was willing to put his own neck on the line to smash Gregory's paedophile ring. Meadows and Okaro know that Hunter can't be trusted and intend keeping a very close eye on him in future.

PC Mike Jarvis

(Stephen Beckett) (1993–8)
Athletic Londoner Mike Jarvis arrived at Sun Hill from Barton Street and developed into a reliable, conscientious officer, his first real complaint arising out of an incident in a rugby match when he was accused of foul play. He took

SUN HILL – *The Facts*

Actor Scott Maslen originally auditioned to play the skinhead sidekick of a fascist in the Sun Hill race riots, but the casting director then asked him to read for the part of DS Phil Hunter.

his job and himself seriously, eventually earning a transfer to the Diplomatic Protection Group.

DI Sally Johnson
(Jaye Griffiths) (1994–5 and 2003–present)
Like Mike Jarvis, Sally Johnson was not lacking in self-belief. Having risen through the ranks at an alarming pace to become a DS at Stafford Row, she was ready to tackle whatever another promotion and Sun Hill could throw at her by way of racist, sexist remarks. Her unshakeable faith in her own abilities irritated a number of more experienced officers and her confidence took a long overdue knock when she was subjected to a private prosecution for manslaughter following the death of drug dealer Lee Ruddick in a police raid. As her methods came under increasing scrutiny, it was clear that her days at Sun Hill were numbered and when she was offered a boring desk job attachment monitoring overtime, she realised she had no choice but to take it.

Trainee DC Brandon Kane
(Pal Aron) (2002–4)
A member of a small Asian family from Leicester, Kane originally trained to be an accountant but by

the time his marriage broke up, he had entered the police service. He spent three years as a PC at another station where CID officers marked him out as a bright, meticulous officer with the potential to become a very good detective. While training for CID at Sun Hill, he has

learned to curb his restless spirit and impulsive nature although this did not prevent him sleeping with the barking mad Cathy Bradford – a move that he would come to regret bitterly.

PC Debbie Keane
(Andrea Mason) (1995–8)
Debbie joined Sun Hill from Hendon along with classmate Nick Slater but soon emerged as the more promising of the two. Having previously worked as an outward bound instructor, she was more

PC Mike Jarvis.

than up to the physical demands of the job while her mature, friendly approach impressed her senior officers, who encouraged her to try for her sergeant's exams. She frequently found herself on the receiving end of Matt Boyden's caustic wit. Searching for a dismembered corpse, she asked: 'How do we know if we've found a bit of body, Sarge?' To which Boyden replied: 'Try chewin' it.'

Sgt. Jane Kendall
(Liz Crowther) (1993)
Born into an RAF family, Jane Kendall joined the police force at 17 and had been a sergeant for four years when she transferred to Sun Hill. An active sportswoman, she was not afraid to be disliked and pull rank in order to get the best performance from those around her. Despite her leadership qualities, her stay was short.

PC Gabriel Kent
(Todd Carty) (2003–present)
Kent is a cop with a criminal record, having been found guilty of assault as a teenager. As he was young and hasn't been in trouble since, the offence wasn't sufficient to prevent him joining the force. Sun Hill is his first posting from Hendon and at first he seemed like a regular guy but in his days in the navy he had a reputation as a bully with a volatile temper and he soon emerged as sly, manipulative, divisive and cruel. He has even managed to obtain a hold over Gina Gold – and that's something that Giant Haystacks would have struggled to do.

Insp. Brian Kite
(Simon Slater) (1987)
An unpopular recruit to the Sun Hill ranks, Kite kept an eagle eye on his relief. He was pedantic, officious and about as compassionate as

Attila the Hun. Choosing to rule by fear, his feminine side was harder to find than a cure for the common cold. Fortunately he didn't stick around too long.

PC Nick Klein
(Rene Zagger) (1999–2004)
Breezy and nonchalant, the only thing that got up Nick Klein's nose was coke. His passion for dance music led to him become a DJ in clubs where drugs were readily available. At first he just indulged in a little recreational grass but as the pressures and temptations grew, he moved onto harder stuff and began to spend a lot of time in toilet cubicles (Hollis no doubt attributed it to the canteen baked beans). Phil Hunter caught him on CCTV and started to make his life hell but Nick got his revenge by uncovering Phil's liaison with the wife of a local hood. An increasingly tortured soul (Cass Rickman once

PC Debbie Keane.

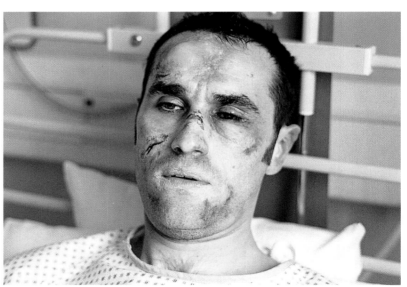

PC Nick Klein.

told him he looked like Dracula with the flu), Nick was finally about to declare his love for her when she fell victim to the Sun Hill serial killer. Klein's drug habit was eventually exposed by Jim Carver and he was sent off to rehab.

DC Duncan Lennox
(George Rossi) (1998–2003)
Big Dunc came to Sun Hill from Epsom at a time when his every move was dictated by the career of his high-flying wife Shona, but when she had an affair and left him he was forced to live in reduced circumstances, a far cry from their luxury riverside apartment. An affable Glaswegian with an ironic sense of humour, he irritated villains by treating them with extreme courtesy. Although he cultivated an image of profound laziness, his mind worked considerably faster than his body and he could suddenly spark into life when scenting the chance of a good arrest. He transferred to MIT early in 2003 to join up with his old boss, Alex Cullen.

DC Alfred 'Tosh' Lines
(Kevin Lloyd) (1988–98)
'Tosh' Lines was Sun Hill's answer to Columbo. A man who always looked as if he had got dressed to the tune of an approaching husband's footsteps, he wore the same suit and scruffy raincoat for weeks on end. He was built like a spacehopper, drove a battered old Volvo, which spent more time in a repair bay than on the road, and

PC Steve Loxton.

his domestic life was, at best, a mess. He had a wife, Muriel, five children and a huge mortgage, and between them, they sapped every penny of his constable's pay. Yet for all that the amiable 'Tosh' was second to none when it came to solving cases, which was why the likes of Burnside were happy to overlook his sartorial short-comings and to protect him from any flak from above. He eventually left Sun Hill to work in the Coroner's Office, a job that happily involved less legwork.

PC Dave Litten
(Gary Olsen) (1983–6)
Ambitious to join CID, Litten took every opportunity to try and impress Roy Galloway. His eager-ness was often misplaced and when he attempted to score Brownie points by taking infor-mation on a series of armed robberies directly to Galloway, he was reprimanded by both the DI and Bob Cryer. Eventually a successful board led to him being temporarily seconded to CID, whereupon he began lording it over his old mates in Uniform. Galloway remained unconvinced.

PC Steve Loxton
(Tom Butcher) (1990–7)
A bit of an enigma was Steve Loxton. In his seven years at Sun Hill, nobody really got to know

SUN HILL – *The Facts*
Rene Zagger (PC Nick Klein) has a Russian/Polish father and a Spanish/Portuguese mother.

him. A former soldier, he came south from Manchester shouting the odds about what a great copper he was. But he also brought with him a racist attitude and an unsympathetic, macho approach that led to public complaints and the mistrust of many of his colleagues. A skilled Area Car driver, at one stage he nurtured ambitions of becoming a firearms officer but in the end he left the force to set up his own security business. Naturally, when he turned up at Dave Quinnan's stag night in 1999 he bragged about what a good career move he had made. The truth was he was up to his ears in debt and booze and was working as a doorman. You just never knew where you were with Steve.

PC Abe Lyttleton

(Ronnie Cush) (1985–6)
The first black officer to be stationed at Sun Hill, Lyttleton was given a hard time by fellow newcomer Pete Muswell who promptly christened him 'Snowball'. Lyttleton rose above Muswell's repeated racist taunts and proved such a capable officer that he even won his tormentor's grudging respect.

DS Debbie McAllister

(Natalie Roles) (2000–present)
Scheming, manipulative but utterly irresistible, McAllister is prepared to do anything to further her career or save her skin. Drafted in from Barton Street as a newly made-up sergeant, she hid the traits of Cruella

SUN HILL – *The Facts*

George Rossi (DC Duncan Lennox) was the chief witness at an Old Bailey murder trial in 1982.

De Vil behind the face of Cinderella. When she was not shafting her colleagues she was getting them to return the favour, but her plans to sleep her way to the top with Tom Chandler backfired when she fell pregnant. Without a maternal bone in her body, she was about to have the baby adopted until Jack Meadows made her think again. For a moment, she almost seemed human.

PC Gary McCann

(Clive Wedderburn) (1992–2000)
Having gained a degree in Politics and History from the University of East Anglia, Gary McCann joined the force as a 'fast-track' graduate. He was always immaculately turned out and because he felt accountable to the black community, he believed in the need to set an example both to the public and to his fellow officers. Intolerant of sloppiness in others, he had an arrogant streak that manifested itself when June Ackland gained promotion at his expense. His elevation to sergeant came along soon enough although it coincided with him being sprayed with CS gas during an ambush.

Sgt. John Maitland

(Sam Miller) (1990–3)
Maitland arrived at Sun Hill under a cloud, having shopped two traffic cops at his previous station for

drinking on duty, but he won the respect of his new colleagues by wading in to rescue Ted Roach from a gang of thugs. Despite being a solid, dependable officer, however, he never topped any popularity charts, being humourless and insistent on doing everything by the book. He left Sun Hill to become an instructor at Hendon.

PC Cathy Marshall

(Lynne Miller) (1989–96)
Cathy Marshall successfully hid a miserable home life (she had been married for ten years to a CID officer who had beaten her up) behind a brisk and efficient desk manner. She arrived fresh from a commendation for single-handedly arresting an armed robber but then opted for a more peaceful life amid the filing cabinets as Sun Hill's collator. Although she had passed her sergeant's exams, she missed life on the beat but her return to pounding the pavements ended in tragedy when she drowned after chasing a suspect into the river.

PC/DC Viv Martella

(Nula Conwell) (1984–93)
Big-hearted Viv was the repeated object of male attention at Sun Hill. The usual suspects – Burnside and Roach – had a go as, more bizarrely, did Tom Penny and Reg

Hollis, but all were rebuffed with a friendly put-down. For Viv had a civvy boyfriend and firmly believed in keeping her private and office lives in separate files. Viv had stranger collars than Harry Hill – she and June Ackland once arrested a man in a bearskin for causing an obstruction – but it was no laughing matter when, an hour later, she failed to prevent a woman jumping to her death from a multi-storey car park. Viv had just applied to join the Bermuda police force but her experience with the jumper left her feeling that she wasn't up to the job and she withdrew her application. After doing a number of undercover operations for CID, it was an inevitable progression for her to switch into plainclothes on a permanent basis. She marked her first day as a detective by tearing her new outfit during a chase. When she arrived back at the nick looking

SUN HILL – *The Facts*

As a teenager, Colin Tarrant (Inspector Andrew Monroe) was a promising footballer and had trials with Huddersfield Town.

more like Worzel Gummidge than Cindy Crawford, a laughing Burnside boomed: 'Welcome to the firm, Viv!' Her career had a tragic ending when building society robbers shot her dead.

DCI Jack Meadows
(Simon Rouse) (1990–present)
A former superintendent with AMIP, Meadows was demoted for lack of supervision over a corruption case but landed on his feet at Sun Hill when Kim Reid was promoted. A tough, seasoned officer who can be brusque but is also not slow in giving praise when it's due, Meadows has gone on to survive a number of crises. He himself faced corruption charges in 1999 and after the

Beech fiasco he was left in no doubt by Chandler that he was in danger of losing his job. However, Chandler had underestimated the enemy and Meadows hung around to haunt – and ultimately destroy – him. Having persuaded Debbie McAllister to keep her baby, Meadows found himself strangely drawn to her. Dumping wife Laura, he made his move, little realising that McAllister would represent an even greater challenge than Chandler.

PC Ken Melvin
(Mark Powley) (1987–90)
Likeable Ken Melvin shocked his fellow officers at Sun Hill by revealing himself to be a Born Again Christian. After all, religion wasn't high on the agenda for canteen conversation, not when there was birds, booze and football to talk about. In May 1990 he was driving a stolen car back to the station when a bomb inside the vehicle exploded. Melvin died later in hospital, the second Sun Hill officer to die within the space of ten months.

Insp. Andrew Monroe
(Colin Tarrant) (1989–2002)
Alec Peters once said of Monroe: 'You don't point Mr Monroe at someone unless you intend to fire

PC Cathy Marshall.

him.' As the new broom with very tough bristles, ex-miner Monroe possessed a frown that could reduce even Brownlow to a quivering wreck. He never needed to raise his voice; he simply put the fear of God into superiors and subordinates alike. Blessed with a flawless knowledge of police procedure, he would, with great politeness, correct anyone who was getting it wrong. Quite simply he was a stickler for detail. Although at work the granite exterior hid a heart of stone, he was rumoured to be a big softy at home and had been happily married for over 20 years until being killed in the station explosion.

DC/DS Jo Morgan
(Mary Jo Randle) (1993–5)
Born in Rochdale, Morgan was transferred to Sun Hill from another tough London district, Hoxton. Confident but headstrong and with little time for social niceties, this ambitious divorcee was a woman in a hurry. She transferred to Regional Crime Squad but her progress slowed to a dead halt when she was gunned down outside the station in October 1995.

Sgt. Sheelagh Murphy
(Bernie Nolan) (2003–present)
The oldest of five children, Sheelagh had to raise her brothers and sisters after her mother died when she was 13. She later moved from her native Ireland to London, where she trained as a nurse before joining the

SUN HILL – The Facts
Lisa Geoghan admits she used to have a crush on her new co-star Todd Carty (PC Gabriel Kent) when they appeared together in the children's drama Tucker's Luck.

police. Sun Hill is her first posting as a sergeant. With three children of her own, ranging from 16 to 20, it was inevitable that the Relief would quickly become another family for Sheelagh, much to the dismay of husband Patrick. Unfortunately she grew a little too close to Des Taviner and ended up pregnant by him.

PC Pete Muswell
(Ralph Brown) (1985–7)
Fresh from battling the flying pickets during the miners' strike, where his indiscriminate use of a truncheon caused the death of a young miner, Muswell arrived at Sun Hill with a hard-man reputation that he enjoyed living up to. Foul-mouthed, bigoted and chauvinistic, he was told by June Ackland that his humour was like his breath! His assertion that rape victims asked for it and probably enjoyed the experience resulted in a washroom brawl with Jim Carver, the latter ending up with a bloodied nose. Few were sorry to see Muswell go.

DS Samantha Nixon
(Lisa Maxwell) (2002–present)
With degrees in Psychology and Criminology, Samantha Nixon tried to join the Met's profiling team but felt that she was turned down for being a woman and a single mum to boot. Her interest in getting under people's skin to discover what makes them tick made many in CID wary of her, but it did enable her to reveal the true identity of the Sun Hill serial killer. Her customary cool was ruffled when she discovered that her 15-year-old daughter Abigail had been sleeping with Matt Boyden, whereupon Nixon strongly advised him to kick the Abi habit. However, Nixon was hiding a secret of her own – that Abigail's father had been convicted of murder at the age of ten. When the news hit the papers, Nixon needed all her composure to stay ahead of the game.

Supt. Adam Okaro
(Cyril Nri) (2002–present)
Okaro had the unenviable job of restoring order at Sun Hill following Chandler's suicide. A principled, civilised human being who had been on the front line during the Brixton riots of 1981, his aptitude for stepping back and assessing the bigger picture set him on an inevitable course towards the top. He became a chief inspector in the West End and moved to Sun Hill after a brief spell as a superintendent at Croydon. A strong leader, he has had to overcome accusations that his rapid promotion had more to do with his colour than his ability.

PC Gemma Osbourne

(Jane Danson) (2002–3)

An energetic member of the Lesbian and Gay Police Association, Gemma set tongues wagging the moment she joined Sun Hill. Always up for what he couldn't have, Des Taviner fancied the pants off her and, to Gemma's amusement, refused to accept that he hadn't a chance in hell. Des tried to pretend he didn't care, once remarking: 'I'd rather have my eyeballs ripped out and dipped in salt than spend another six hours in the Area Car with her.' Hell hath no fury like a macho man scorned. Gemma served her probation with Greater Manchester Constabulary (having her first love-job relationship with an older sergeant) before joining the Met's Traffic Patrol. She excelled at Sun Hill until a brutal attack led to her going off the rails completely. After helping an asylum seeker to escape from detention and verbally abusing Gina Gold, she was sent for a brain scan and was pronounced unfit for duty.

PC Polly Page

(Lisa Geoghan) (1992–2004)

Everybody loved Polly. The chirpy Cockney with a mission to clean up the streets of London proved herself a brave officer with a firm social conscience. She was somebody to depend on when the going got tough. But the one thing always missing in her life was a steady man. In 1998 she fell for a conman and never forgave John Boulton for using her to get a result. Tony Stamp wanted to get closer but she couldn't see him as anything more than a friend and turned him down in favour of the emotional minefield that was Dave Quinnan. Polly has never been the same since. Predictably their affair ended in tears and Polly had to take sick leave to recover from Quinnan's decision to quit Sun Hill. But things were no better when she returned, and she took an overdose on the night that the station went up in flames, as a result of which Ackland put her on long-term leave. She returned a year later as part of the CSU and befriended a doctor with a brain tumour. When the doctor died, Polly was charged with murder. Although innocent, she had made the mistake of letting the cover-up queen, Cathy Bradford, talk her into concealing the truth.

PC Danesh Patel

(Sonesh Sira) (1987)

Patel was a young Asian officer who came to Sun Hill at a time when there were an increasing number of attacks on Asian families in the area. Despite receiving kindly encouragement from Bob Cryer, Patel failed to last the pace.

DS Danny Pearce

(Martin Marquez) (1993–5)

Pearce was Essex man through and through – the gold watch, the flash suits, the hint of cockiness and the list of contacts in the sporting world. Transferred from Romford, he desperately tried to ingratiate himself with DI Sally Johnson but found Chris Deakin a tougher nut to crack. Deakin was impressed with results not empty boasts and Pearce's star appeared to be on the wane until he joined AMIP.

Sgt. Tom Penny

(Roger Leach) (1984–90)

Even Bob Cryer found Tom Penny hard work. A miserable so and so, he took out his frustrations by beating his wife. His world began to crumble in 1988 when he was shot in the stomach while investigating a complaint and numbed the pain by consuming copious amounts of alcohol. He returned to the job but was clearly under mental strain and eventually confided to Cryer that he had a drink problem. Driving home from the party to mark Cryer's 20 years' service, he was stopped, breathalysed and found to be over the limit. His reputation ruined, he decided that the best course was to resign on medical grounds, citing the old gunshot wound.

Sgt. Alec Peters

(Larry Dann) (1984–92)

SUN HILL – *The Facts*

Lisa Maxwell (DI Samantha Nixon) was originally lined up to play Daphne in Frasier but lost 'the role of a lifetime' to Jane Leeves after telling the show's writer it was 'very unfunny'.

By contrast to Tom Penny, his fellow sergeant Alec Peters was a jovial sort, not averse to sharing a laugh and a joke with the Relief. But like Penny's his health and career went downhill after he was the victim of violence – in Peters' case a kid high on drugs stabbed him in the stomach. The incident had such a profound effect on him that he was moved 'upstairs' to a desk job where he could quietly see out the remaining years to his retirement.

DC Tom Proctor

(Gregory Donaldson) (1997–2000)
Sadly, Tom Proctor's detection methods owed more to Clouseau than Poirot. If there was a bungled operation, the chances were that Proctor was somehow responsible. Rod Skase took great delight in tormenting his naïve young

Sgt Tom Penny.

colleague and after one cock-up too many, the hapless Proctor was transferred to Isleworth CSU – his worst nightmare.

PC Dave Quinnan

(Andrew Paul) (1989–2002)
A charmer and wind-up merchant rolled into one, Dave was always first to the bar and the first to lend a colleague a tenner if they were short. He was everybody's best mate – until he was brutally attacked by a gang of youths in 1999. Recovering in St. Hugh's, he fell for a nurse, Jenny, who also happened to be George Garfield's girlfriend. Dave and Jenny got married but it didn't work out, partly because Dave was having an affair with Polly Page. Dave lost his marbles as well as his wife and had to take two months' sick leave. Scarred by his experiences, he was never again the same happy-go-lucky Dave and with Sun Hill holding too many bad memories, he decided to accept a job at SO10.

PC Pete Ramsey

(Nick Reding) (1988–9)
Porsche-driving Pete Ramsey used his uniform to throw his weight about and impress girls. Arrogant and irresponsible, he had run-ins with a number of his colleagues, including the upright Ken Melvin, whom he horrified by driving their patrol car at some children 'for a bit of sport'. Ironically the man who lived life as a nasty bastard died a hero's death, shot while

protecting 'Tosh' Lines during a bank robbery. It was probably the lowest turn-out for a funeral in the history of Sun Hill.

DC Liz Rawton

(Libby Davison) (1996–9)
Newcastle-born Liz Rawton joined Sun Hill from SO11 (criminal intelligence), where she honed her skills in surveillance and undercover operations. Preferring to use brains than brawn, she was unfazed by the laddish antics of CID and could deliver a look as severe as her hair-cut. Her talents were recognised when she was posted to Serious Crime Group, where, on a return to Tyneside, she helped Burnside bust a bent DCI. She has since left the force to work as a private investigator.

DCI Kim Reid

(Carolyn Pickles) (1990–2)
Kim Reid arrived at Sun Hill in style – with a sandwich in one hand and a prisoner in the other. If Frank Burnside thought a woman boss would be an easy touch, he soon found that it didn't pay to underestimate her and she proceeded to win over her new charges with her resilience and humour. She knew full well that her performance was being monitored by those in high places and indeed her next promotion was not long in coming. Moving on to MS15 (Internal Investigations), she briefly returned to Sun Hill to look into a complaint of sexual assault against George Garfield.

PC Cass Rickman

(Suzanne Maddock) (1999–2002)
Cass Rickman worked hard and played hard, devoting as much energy to police duties as she did to her favourite pastime of clubbing. The young Scouser was quick-witted and feisty with a tendency to open her mouth without thinking but her blunt honesty meant that nobody took offence for long. Sam Harker and Nick Klein both fancied her but she had lousy taste in men, preferring the company of criminal Leroy Jones, who once took her on a bank robbery. Not surprisingly, that episode threatened her career but it took Pat Kitson, the Sun Hill serial killer, to end it.

DC Paul Riley

(Gary Grant) (2000–2)
With less charisma than the average police baton, Paul Riley blended in so well on his arrival at Sun Hill from Barton Street that few people knew he was there. Laid-back to the point of being almost comatose, he was easy prey for the Machiavellian wiles of Debbie McAllister but his biggest problem was his dodgy brother, Joe, who was forever getting into scrapes. Even so, Joe couldn't be blamed for the petrol bomb that took Paul's life.

DS Ted Roach

(Tony Scannell) (1984–93)
A wild, boozy Irishman who got into more fights than Lennox Lewis, Ted Roach became a legend at Sun Hill. Both Galloway and Burnside rated Roach as a thief-taker but his unpredictable behaviour was a constant source of concern to Brownlow, who ensured that he would never rise above detective sergeant. Not that Ted needed any help, turning up for one promotion board with blood streaming from his brow after being head-butted in the pub. This lack of advancement made Ted bitter, and when Ted was under stress he hit the Scotch. He had a lot of stress. After one drunken brawl too many he punched Inspector Monroe in the face and, refusing to apologise, walked out of the job. Seven years on he was living in a flat above a massage parlour and still boozing. It was probably the same binge. Never fussy about his women, he was now involved with an old snout, a transvestite called Roxanne, but she died in his arms after being stabbed. Ted might just have needed a drink to get over that.

PC Pete Ramsay.

PC Eddie Santini

(Michael Higgs) (1998–2000)
Fast Eddie Santini was bad news. At first he had the air of a harmless Italian Romeo but it soon transpired that he was about as safe to know as a Mafia hitman. He subjected PC Rosie Fox to a sustained campaign of sexual harassment and succeeded in turning the entire nick against her. Devious and dangerous, he found a soul-mate in Vicky Hagen, who did her best to bail him out when he was charged with murdering his part-time lover, Jessica Orton. Santini was acquitted but by now he was in deep with the wrong people and he was finally gunned down in his flat.

DC Eva Sharpe
(Diane Parish) (2002–2004)
A straightforward working-class girl, Sharpe may not be the brightest academically but she has a good radar for what makes people tick. Married to an environmental health officer (they have two children), she uses her colour to her advantage and deals with whatever racism she encounters in the job in the same way that she deals with everything else in life – head on. She suffered every mother's nightmare when daughter Joanna went missing. No sooner had she recovered from that ordeal then she was wrongly accused over a death in custody.

PC Nick Shaw
(Chris Walker) (1985–7)
The burly northerner was not a guy to mess with. Although he did have a caring side, he was at his happiest in the pub swapping tales of bravado with his mates. He was a good, conscientious copper and displayed his frustration at being wrongly accused of pocketing fines by losing his temper with his CIB interro-gators. It was not a shrewd career move and he left Sun Hill shortly afterwards.

DS Vik Singh
(Raji James) (2000–2)
Hyperactive and cocky, Singh was a techno-logical whiz kid who was sometimes too clever for his own good. His downfall came after he had been the victim of racial taunts, as a result of which he put a suspected white suprem-acist in hospital – a lack of discipline that would have disastrous and tragic effects for Sun Hill. Suspended by Meadows pending a CIB investigation, he chose to resign with immediate effect rather than face the music.

DC Rod Skase
(Iain Fletcher) (1994–2000).
Swaggering Skase thought he knew it all. In his mind he ran CID, although more often than not his overwhelming self-confidence left him with egg on his face. With his sharp suits and slicked-back hair, he reckoned he was God's gift to women as well as to the job but his arrogance and caustic wit meant that he turned more stomachs than heads. In the end his pride came before a spectacular fall. When it emerged that he had bullied a witness into lying in order to get a result, Skase chose to walk before Meadows could sack him or have him charged with perverting the course of justice. Hot Rod was out in the cold.

PC Nick Slater
(Alan Westaway) (1995–7)
With his boyish looks, Nick Slater didn't look old enough to be allowed out on night patrols. A former salesman, he had a healthy disrespect for authority but still looked up to the seasoned veterans at Sun Hill. Tony Stamp took him under his wing but frequently despaired of the new boy's foolishness. Despite his undeniable enthusiasm, he was never quite cut out for the rough stuff. Anyway he probably had a note from his mum. Left to join SO10.

PC/Sgt. Dale Smith
(Alex Walkinshaw) (1999–2001, 2003–present)
The product of a dysfunctional London family, former squaddie Smithy saw himself as Sun Hill's version of Action Man. While he was

DC Rod Skase.

definitely someone to count on in a tight situation, his hard-line attitude alienated a number of his colleagues, who considered him to be narrow-minded and bigoted. Following a spell with SO19 (marked by the accidental shooting of his mentor, Bob Cryer), he returned to Sun Hill as a sergeant in 2003. In his new role he is loyal to his troops but hates anyone who doesn't take responsibility for their actions or back up their fellow officers. Cryer's faith in him has been justified.

PC Tony 'Yorkie' Smith

(Robert Hudson) (1984–9)
Barely recovered from being slashed while infiltrating a gang of soccer hooligans, 'Yorkie' Smith stumbled across a seemingly routine road traffic accident, but with fatalities, two feuding drivers and no back-up, he rapidly lost control of the situation. Admitting that he had struggled to cope, this once dependable officer decided to leave the force and go into the security business. However, he became restless and rejoined the police, and by 1992 had risen to become a DC in his homeland of South Yorkshire.

PC Ron Smollett

(Nick Stringer) (1990–3)
Every station needs a Ron Smollett. Twenty years in Traffic Division meant that he knew the patch like the back of his hand and he never forgot a face, which made him a useful collator at Sun Hill. But soon he grew restless and

SUN HILL – *The Facts*

Alex Walkinshaw, who plays Sgt Dale Smith, appeared three times in The Bill in his teens and was arrested each time.

PC 'Yorkie' Smith.

volunteered to become Home Beat Officer on the notorious Kingsmead Estate. Although his community police station was blown up within a few months, it took more than a bomb to deter an old school copper like Smollett.

DC Kate Spears

(Tania Emery) (2000–2)
First impressions suggested that

Kate Spears was an airhead who would have been more suited to a nightclub than a police station. But the committed party girl and product of a broken home was far from being innocent, ingenuous or a soft touch. She was bold, confident, passionate and quick to dissipate the girly image when expressing her commitment to the job. Her looks did not go unnoticed by Chandler and they embarked on a dangerous affair which ended hours before Spears died in hospital following the petrol bomb attack on Sun Hill.

PC Tony Stamp

(Graham Cole) (1988–present)

Tony Stamp loves his job…but then he must do considering that he has been shot at, stabbed, beaten up half a dozen times, tried for causing death by dangerous driving and accused of child abuse. He was cleared of the last two charges but the experiences caused him to reassess his life and question the abilities of his superior officers. Raised in Slough, Stamp opted for the excitement of working for the Met and hasn't been disappointed. He has never been ambitious and sees policing as more about making arrests and patrolling the front line than protecting the community. Consequently he sometimes lacks tact when dealing with the public. He can also be a bear with a sore head around the station, for whilst outwardly friendly he is deeply lonely and desperate to find a good policewoman. Cagney, Lacey, Polly Page, he doesn't mind.

DS Claire Stanton

(Clara Salaman) (1999–2000)

When Stanton arrived from Finchley, CID were told that she chose Sun Hill because her mother, who lived in the area, had recently suffered a stroke. But the truth was that she had been sent

PC Barry Stringer.

by CIB to spy on Don Beech. Unfortunately, her clandestine investigation into Beech became compromised by her affair with John Boulton, following whose murder she became more determined than ever to nail desperate Don. Even after she quit the force to work in security, she made it her mission to bring Beech to justice.

Sgt. Ray Steele
(Robert Perkins) (1993–6)
A tough recruit from Barton Street, Steele had a snarling presence that caused some of his colleagues to question how far he would go if riled. These doubts multiplied when an old lag died in the cells at Sun Hill and the finger of suspicion was pointed at Steele. He was exonerated after it transpired that the victim had died from a heart attack but the episode had made him realise who his friends were – and they were so few as to be considered an endangered species.

PC Barry Stringer
(Jonathan Dow) (1990–3)
The unassuming, liberal-minded Brummie had none of the hang-ups that beset some of his fellow officers and treated everyone the same regardless of colour or sex.

He became a popular figure around Sun Hill but as the new Federation rep (he beat Hollis by 58 votes to two) he grew disillusioned with life on the beat and the undermanning of PCs. When he contested the latest ban on overtime, it was suggested that he apply for promotion.

Chief Insp. Paul Stritch
(Mark Spalding) (1995)
A chief inspector at 35, Stritch was Philip Cato's short-term replacement at Sun Hill, transferring from Scotland Yard where he lectured senior officers on the issue of public order. Stritch continued to deliver lectures on his first day at Sun Hill until Derek Conway took him to one side for a quiet word. From then on the two men reached an understanding, although Stritch's policies were never well received.

PC Cameron Tait
(Daniel MacPherson) (2003–present)
After being mistaken for a flasher by a neighbour and investigated by Kerry Young, things could only get better for the station's handsome young Aussie recruit. Tait's cheerful, sunny nature masks a deep-seated resentment. He loved being a cop in Australia but struggles to adjust

to life in England, a country he clearly dislikes with some intensity. Then it emerges that he has a secret child. Maybe Tait isn't so clean-cut after all.

PC Des Taviner
(Paul Usher) (2001–4)
A womaniser and a bigot, Taviner was an Area Car driver with an inflated sense of his own importance. Chandler took an immediate dislike to him (they were at Hendon together) and the rest of the Relief were not far behind. The exception was Reg Hollis and the pair teamed up to become The Unlikely Lads. Fearless of authority, it was Taviner who lobbed the fateful petrol bomb into Sun Hill to destroy some counterfeit £50 notes. Wracked with guilt, he later tried to commit suicide but was talked out of it by Hollis, who decided not to reveal his secret to his superiors on the grounds that Taviner had already suffered enough. Despite the fact that he had wiped out half a dozen officers, Taviner could be an asset to the force, bravely rescuing a boy from a burning car in 2002. But a dangerous liaison with Sheelagh Murphy and the very real threat of exposure over the petrol bombing finally unhinged him. After trying to take his own life, he was murdered in his Sun Hill cell by a fellow prisoner.

PC Richard Turnham
(Chris Humphreys) (1989–90)
Sun Hill was merely a lowly rung on Turnham's ladder to the top.

SUN HILL – *The Facts*
Graham Cole is a former Butlin's Redcoat. He met his future wife Cherry when, as a 16-year-old holidaymaker, she won the beauty contest at the Camber Sands camp.

DC Alan Woods.

ambitions, Mickey Webb made no secret of his desire to become a DS. Essex born and bred, he transferred to Sun Hill from Porter's Avenue near Dagenham, hoping to carve out a reputation as a thief-taker. He could be cocky and ruthless and was not afraid to go it alone in order to reach his goals, proving himself when infiltrating a gang of football hooligans. The likes of Kate Spears and Robbie Cryer had been known to fall for his rough charm but any woman would automatically have come second to Mickey's love for his own reflection. However Mickey's jokey nature took a severe jolt when he was raped, as a result of which he decided to walk out on CID.

DC Alan Woods
(Tom Cotcher) (1992–6)
The unruffled Glaswegian provided an island of calm in the stormy seas of Sun Hill CID. An effective detective with an unblemished record, Woods had nothing to prove, unlike some of the more zealous younger members of the department. Unfortunately for Woods, these included his new DI, Sally Johnson, whom he viewed with deep suspicion. More comfortable in a male working environment, he was quietly pleased when Chris Deakin replaced her.

PC Di Worrell
(Jane Wall) (1999–2002)
Raised in Stratford, East London,

Cambridge educated (his father worked in the Home Office, his mother was a GP), the only blot on his copybook was an affair with the chief super's wife at Bow St. Such a scandal might have damaged most careers but with Turnham's connections even that could not prevent a successful application to join Special Branch.

DC Mickey Webb
(Chris Simmons) (2000–3)
Short in stature but with lofty

close to Sun Hill, Di Worrell sought her first posting away from the area to avoid bumping into old schoolfriends on the beat but as she grew in confidence she felt able to move back closer to home. Intuitive and with an impish sense of humour, she was tougher than she looked although she was unable to survive the petrol bomb blast that rocked Sun Hill in 2002.

DCI Gordon Wray
(Clive Wood) (1990)
Born in Windsor in 1947, university-educated Wray joined the force in 1971, serving five years in his home town before joining the Met. Wray was married to a senior social worker, and he arrived at Sun Hill with a glowing reputation and a mandate to clamp down on the errant Frank Burnside. Ironically Burnside quickly saw off his nemesis as Wray proved more human and flawed than anyone had imagined, falling for the hitherto hidden charms of June Ackland. When their affair became the main item of station gossip, Wray was hastily transferred and his hopes of future promotion wrecked.

PC Kerry Young
Beth Cordingly, 2002–present)
Anyone who chases and arrests a mugger while wearing her bridal dress is a force to be reckoned with. Step forward Kerry Young. Sparky and gregarious, Kerry arrived at Sun Hill as a young woman living life to the full. Raised single-handedly by

PC Phil Young.

her doting father (her mother died when she was four), Kerry believed in fairytale romances, unaware that her Prince Charming, Luke Ashton, was bisexual. When the penny finally dropped, Kerry dropped Luke, but not before she had been through a marriage and a miscarriage. Not surprisingly, she has lost a little of her natural bounce.

PC Phil Young
(Colin Alldridge) (1990–1)

Troubled Phil Young cracked up after discovering the body of a 15-year-old girl who had committed suicide. He was always too sensitive for such a demanding job, and when he reached out for help to Norika Datta, he sexually assaulted her after she rejected his advances. By now Young had completely lost it and when he came across another suicide it was too much for him and he took his own life by feeding exhaust fumes into his car.

Index

England, Karen 51
ethnic issues 17, 27, 85, 91–4

Fallon, Howard 73, 74, 75
Family Affairs 126
Ferdinand, Joseph 82, 83
Ferguson, John 58–9, 61
Finnessey, Chris 86–7
Fish 130
Fitzwilliam, Jane 111–12
Fletcher, Iain see Skase, Rod
Floyd, Russell see Drummond, Ken
Flying Squad 55
Ford, Suzanne (Vikki Gee-Dare) 146–7
Fox, Rosie 12, 56–8, 59, 61, 160
Frank, Angela 147
Frank, Robin (Ashley Gunstock) 147
Frasier 157
Frazer, Christine (Barbara Thorn) 30, 31–2, 33, 37, 138, 143, 147, 150
French, Delia (Natasha Williams) 147, 148
Fullerton, Harry 94, 96

Gaffney, Dean 130
Galloway, Roy (John Salthouse) 22–3, 22–4, 159
    attitude to women 22
    moves on 27, 30
    profile 147
    reprimands Litten 27, 153–4
    road rage of 22
Galloway, Roy (Robert Pugh) (in the pilot show Woodentop) 27, 104, 147
Garfield, George (Huw Higginson) 53, 62, 63–5, 67, 149, 159
    beaten up by burglar 50–1
    profile 147–48
    quarrels with Quinnan over nurse Jenny Delaney 65–6, 158
Garrard 75
gay love scenes 15, 16–17, 101
Gee-Dare, Vikki see Ford, Suzanne
Geoghan, Lisa see Page, Polly
Gilmore, Craig (Hywel Simons) 16–17
    affair with Luke Ashton 101, 106, 110, 138, 148
    and Des Taviner 89–90, 91
    and Matt Boyden 97
    presses for transfer 110–11
    profile 148
Give Us a Break 10–11
Glaze, Danny (Karl Collins) 74, 91–3, 96, 115, 148
Glover, Mick 63–4
Gold, Gina (Roberta Taylor) 14, 98, 110–11, 117, 148, 152, 157
Gold, Richard 148
Goodwin, Trudie see Ackland, June
Graham, Marie 117-18
Grant, Gary see Riley, Paul
Grant, Martin 45
Grantham, Leslie 132
Gregory, Ron 111, 113–14, 150
Greig, Alistair 45, 148
Griffiths, Ciaran see Best, Gary
Griffiths, Jaye see Johnson, Sally
Gunstock, Ashley see Frank, Robin

Haddigan, Mark see Able, Timothy
Hagen, Vicky (Samantha Robson) 58, 59, 61, 62, 85–6, 140, 148–9, 160
Haines, Harry (Gary Whelan) 149
Haines, Robert 81
Handford, Richard 105
Hanson, Paul Page 51
Harker, Sam (Matthew Crompton) 65, 94, 95, 149, 159
Harman, Honey (Kim Tiddy) 129, 149
Harrap (Hugh Laurie) 132
Harris, Donna (Louise Harrison) 149
Harris (robber) 38
Harrison, Louise see Harris, Donna
Hartley, Steven see Chandler, Tom
Hawkes, Chesney 132
Haynes, Malcolm (Eamonn Walker) 149–50
Hayward, Ben (Ben Peyton) 95, 143, 150
Helen (girlfriend of Hollis) 90
Higginson, Huw see Garfield, George
Higgs, Michael see Santini, Eddie
Hodges (CIB boss) 72, 75
Holby City 14
Hollis, Reg (Jeff Stewart) 10, 15, 26, 38, 53, 61, 67, 95, 106, 130,

132, 134, 146, 153, 155, 163
    accused of the murder of Doreen Tyler 87–8
    driven into burning building by Taviner 115
    interview with Jeff Stewart 28–9
    Jeff's role in Crossroads 28
    kidnapping of 29, 100–1
    paired with Des Taviner 89–90, 91, 150, 163–4
    popularity 29
    profile 150
Holloway, Annie 42
Holm, Lisa (Alex Kingston) 132
Holmes, Kerry (Joy Brook) 150
homophobia 97, 148
Hudson, Robert see Smith, Tony 'Yorkie'
Humphreys, Chris see Turnham, Richard
Hunter, Cindy 111, 113, 114
Hunter, Phil (Scott Maslen) 97, 106, 107, 111–12, 122-3,153
    and the paedophile ring 113–14, 150
    profile 150–1
Hyde, Connie see Bradford, Cathy

Iles, Jon see Dashwood, Mike
Independent Television (ITV) 11, 12, 13
Indrani, Seeta see Datta, Norika
Ingram, Rob 96
Internal Investigations (MS15) 102, 159
international appeal of The Bill 14
Inverdale, Clive 112–13

Jackson, Kit 18
Jakes, Terry (Dean Gaffney) 130
James, Raji see Singh, Vik
Janice (Emma Bunton) 130
Janie (informant) 63–4
Jarvis, Mike (Stephen Beckett) 151
Jasmine Allen Estate 91, 147
Jayasundera, Thusitha see De Costa, Ramani
Johnjo (drunk) 69, 70
Johnson, Sally (Jaye Griffiths) 53, 145, 157, 165
    profile 151
    trial of 47–8, 49–50
Jones, Leroy 88–9, 159

Kane, Brandon (Pal Aron) 98, 99, 109, 110, 140, 151–2
Keane, Debbie (Andrea Mason) 71, 152
Kemp, Martin 132
Kendall, Jane (Liz Crowther) 152
Kent, Gabriel (Todd Carty) 14, 117-19, 152, 156
Kincaid, Joe 110, 111
Kingsley, Hilary (author) 11
Kingston, Alex 132
Kite, Brian (Simon Slater) 27, 30, 147, 152
Kitson, Pat 108, 109, 159
Kitson, Simon 106, 107, 108–9
Klein, Nick (Rene Zagger) 41, 90, 106, 107–8, 109
    attracted to Cass Rickman 159
    drug taking/clubbing lifestyle of 96–7, 152–3
    profile 152–3
    sleeps with Kerry Young 98
Knock, The 127
Knowles, Terry 90–1
Kray twins 89

Laurie, Hugh 132
Lawson, Charlie 29
Leach, Roger see Penny, Tom
Leeves, Jane 157
Lehmann, Melanie (Denise Van Outen) 132
Lennie (car thief) 24–5
Lennox, Duncan (Rossi, George) 65, 78, 109, 153, 154
Lennox, Shona 153
Lesbian and Gay Police Association 157
Lewson, David (Fish) 130
Lindsay, Robert 11
Lines, Alfred 'Tosh' (Kevin Lloyd) 13, 27, 31, 33, 35, 38, 40, 47, 105, 147, 158
    fitness of 45
    profile 153
Lines, Muriel 35, 153
Litten, Dave (Gary Olsen) 104
    ambition 26–7
    blunders/mistakes of 27
    profile 153–4
Lloyd, Kevin see Lines, Alfred 'Tosh'
location of The Bill 11

London's Burning 127
Lovell 44
Loxton, Steve (Tom Butcher) 37, 154
Lusardi, Linda see Lyons, Maggie
Lynette (dancer) 74
Lyons, Maggie (Linda Lusardi) 132, 139
Lyttleton, Abe (Ronnie Cush) 27, 154

McAllister, Debbie (Natalie Roles) 43, 69, 83–4, 95, 101, 159
    affair with Tom Chandler 95, 96, 100, 102–3
    gives birth to baby boy 106, 154
    Jack Meadows' romantic interest in 112, 154, 155
    marriage to Tom Chandler 103, 142, 154
    profile 154
McGann, Gary (Clive Wedderburn) 17, 86, 154
McGann, Paul 11
Mackenzie, Jack (Ray Winstone) 43
MacPherson, Daniel see Tait, Cameron
McQueen, Geoff (writer) 10–11
Maddock, Suzanne see Rickman, Cass
Magnum, Thomas 98
Maitland, John (Sam Miller) 154
Mannion, Guy 75, 142
Marchant, Tony 104
Marion (Brownlow's secretary) 141
Marquess, Paul (producer) 11–17
Marquez, Martin see Pearce, Danny
Marsden, Louise 100, 102
Marsden, Peter 96, 100, 102
Marsh, Tom (Martin Kemp) 132
Marshall, Cathy (Lynne Miller) 37, 154–7
Martella, Viv (Nula Conwell) 27, 46, 155
Mary (fiancée of 'Taffy' Edwards) 146
Maslen, Scott see Hunter, Phil
Mason, Andrea see Keane, Debbie
Massie, Jimmy 132
Massie, Patrick (Rik Mayall) 132
Maxwell, Lisa see Nixon, Samantha
Mayall, Rik 132
Meadows, Jack (Simon Rouse) 36, 41, 47, 57, 68, 75, 93, 115, 149, 150–1, 160
    appointed DCI 44, 45
    attitude to women 42–3
    and Chandler's downfall 96, 100, 102, 103, 142
    corruption of 44
    in crisis 78–9
    interview with Simon Rouse 42–3
    and Johnson's trial 48, 49–50
    and the paedophile ring 112, 113
    and Phil Hunter 111
    profile 155
    romantic interest in Debbie McAllister 112, 154, 155
    sees prostitute after marital break up 114
Meadows, Laura 42, 112, 115, 155
Melanie (Jaime Murray) 99
Melvin, Ken (Mark Powley) 35, 155–6, 158
Merrick, Anne 101–2
Merseybeat 16
Merton 11
Metropolitan Police 17, 24, 55
Miller, Lynne see Marshall, Cathy
Miller, Sam see Maitland, John
MIT 17
MIT 95–6, 100, 109, 144, 153
Mitchell, Carl 52
Monroe, Andrew (Colin Tarrant) 37, 38, 47, 49, 51, 62, 66, 68, 70, 94, 95, 155, 156, 159
Moore, Larry (Roger Daltrey) 130
Morgan, Jo (Mary Jo Randle) 52, 156
Morris, Claudia 47, 48
Mr Gay UK contest 127
MS15 (Internal Investigations) 102, 159
Murphy, Patrick 156
Murphy, Sheelagh (Bernie Nolan) 14, 115, 156, 164
Murray, Billy see Beech, Don
Muswell, Pete (Ralph Brown) 27, 154, 156
National Crime Squad 89, 141
National Youth Theatre 104
Neal, Scott see Ashton, Luke
Neighbours 126
News International 11
Nguyen, Frankie 89
night shoots 19
Nixon, Abigail (Georgia Moffett) 108, 140, 156
Nixon, Samantha (Lisa Maxwell) 109, 140, 156, 157